MUSLIM AND CHRISTIAN
GRANADA

A COMPLETE GUIDE TO THE ALHAMBRA AND CHRISTIAN
MONUMENTS OF GRANADA INCLUDING MAPS AND MORE
THAN 160 ORIGINAL PHOTOGRAPHS AND DRAWINGS

Published by EDILUX S.L.
Editor: J. Agustín Núñez
Original text: Aurelio Cid Acedo
English translation: Jon Trout
Photographs: Miguel Román and J. Agustín Núñez
Photographic composition: EDILUX S.L.
Layout, design and drawings: Miguel Salvatierra
Map of Granada: Xavier Bosch
Map on page 5: Ignacio Belda
Printing: Copartgraf s.c.a.
Binding: Hermanos Olmedo s.l.
ISBN: 84-95856-07-7
L.D.: GR-818-2002

© EDILUX S.L.
© diagrams and drawings: Miguel Salvatierra
e-mail: edilux@supercable.es
Tlf: 958-082000

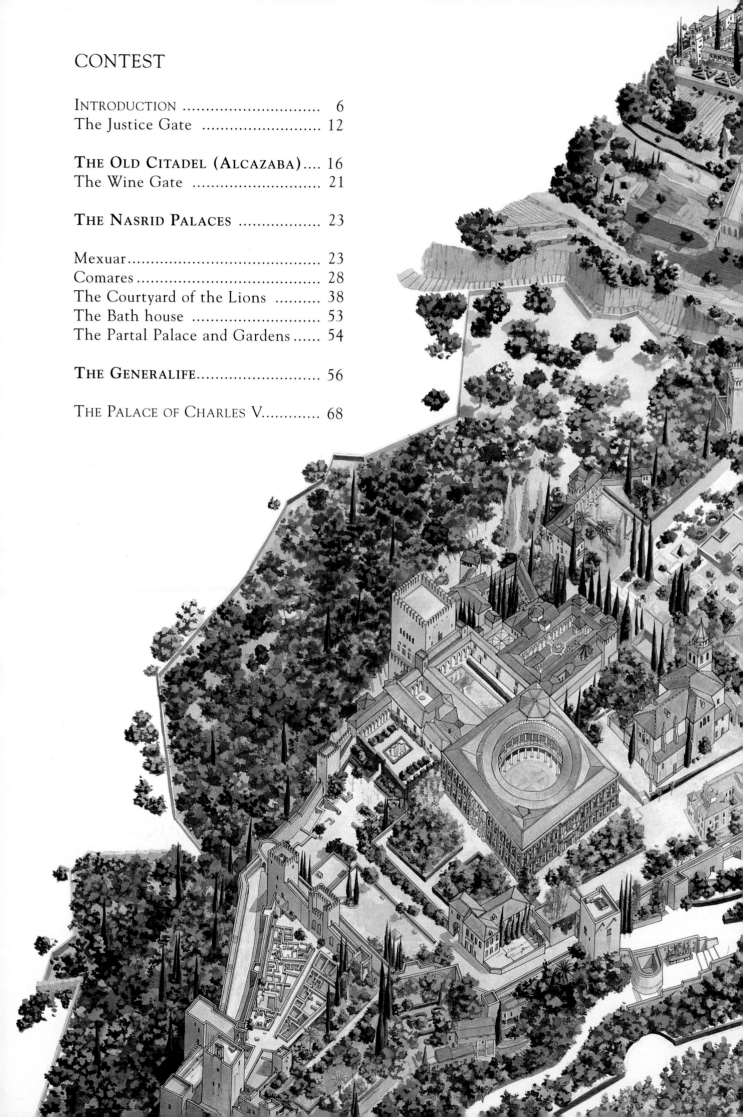

CONTEST

Dibujo de Nacho Belda

Río Darro

Cuesta de los Chinos

JARDINES DEL PARTAL

PALACIOS NAZARÍES

PALACIO de CARLOS V

ALCAZABA

Puerta de la Justicia

Puerta del Vino

Acceso peatonal desde Cuesta de Gomérez

P

TICKETS
ENTRADA

LA ALHAMBRA

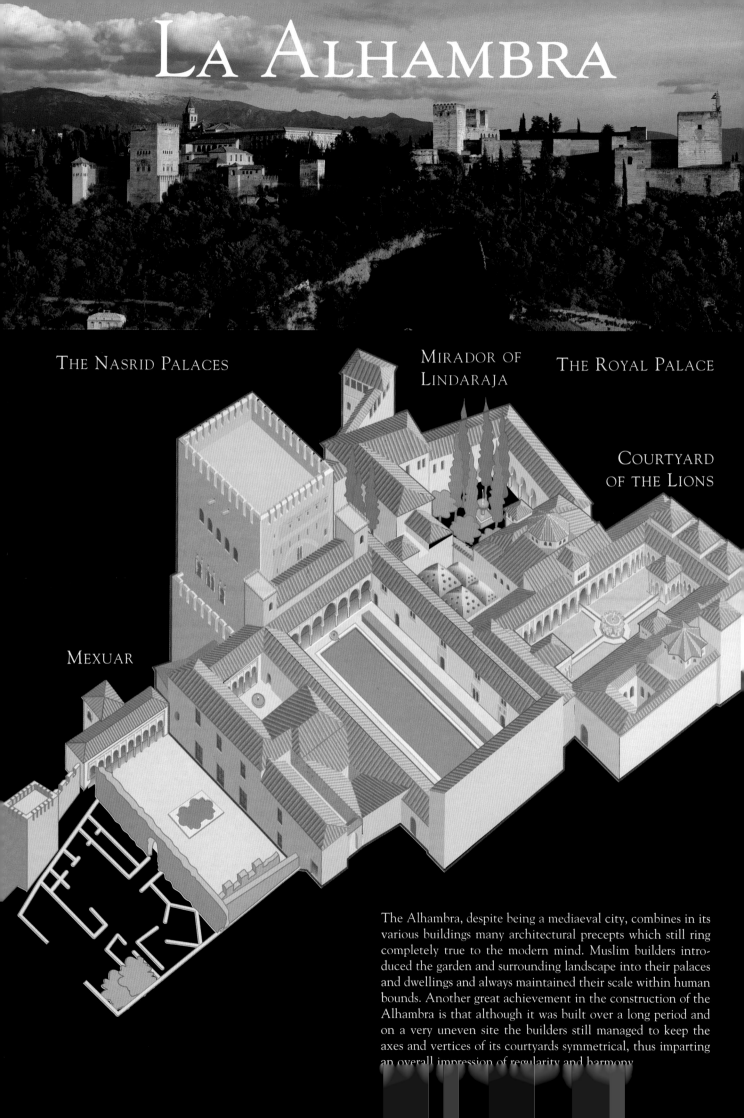

THE NASRID PALACES

MIRADOR OF LINDARAJA

THE ROYAL PALACE

COURTYARD OF THE LIONS

MEXUAR

The Alhambra, despite being a mediaeval city, combines in its various buildings many architectural precepts which still ring completely true to the modern mind. Muslim builders introduced the garden and surrounding landscape into their palaces and dwellings and always maintained their scale within human bounds. Another great achievement in the construction of the Alhambra is that although it was built over a long period and on a very uneven site the builders still managed to keep the axes and vertices of its courtyards symmetrical, thus imparting an overall impression of regularity and harmony.

INTRODUCTION

The royal city of the Alhambra stands proudly above Granada upon the hill known in the middle ages as the Cerro de la Sabika, the Hill of Gold. It is one of the most important architectural structures of the Middle Ages in Spain and the finest example of Islamic architecture left to us in the western world.

The steep scarp upon which the Alhambra stands forms a rough triangle; at its eastern end is the Cerro del Sol (Hill of the Sun), beneath which nestles the Generalife, the private retreat of the Nasrid royalty, and a small fortress known as the Seat of the Moor. Running beneath its abrupt northern flank is the valley of the river Darro; at its western extreme stands the Alcazaba citadel and to the south runs a deep valley separating the Alhambra proper from the Mauror Hill and the Vermilion Towers, where a path climbs through woods to the gates of the Muslim citadel. The hill is composed of reworked detritus from the Sierra Nevada, mainly schists and quartz, deposited some six million years ago in an alluvial fan delta. Subsequent tectonic activity left it staggered into four distinct terraces, the Alhambra itself standing on the third one down. The deposits are in fact grey, the distinctive red colour which gives the hill its name being due to a thin covering of oxidised palaeosoil. At its highest point it is some seven hundred metres above sea level.. The shape of the whole citadel resembles that of a boat with its prow, the Alcazaba, set on a tireless course towards the city. It is seven hundred metres from its stem, the Alcazaba, to its stern, the Cabo de la Carrera tower, and two hundred metres in the beam at its widest. In all it covers an area of some thirteen hectares and is enclosed by more than two kilometres of walls reinforced by some thirty towers, many of which are now in ruins.

The Alhambra has not always been appreciated for the architecture itself. We all seem to become mere tourists in the Alhambra. A group of Spanish architects wrote in 1953 in the Manifiesto de la Alhambra that "The Alhambra is a monument that has never been looked at properly from an architectural point of view; it is curious: not even by those architects who sharpen their professional eye (if we might put it like that) before the Escorial; when they come to the Alhambra they let go the reins of their critical perspicacity to become tourists like any other, even to the extent of excusing their complacency by alleging a clear distinction as far as their emotions are concerned: Yes, I like this a lot, but not as architecture." Later in the same text they add, "The relationship between this building of the XIV century and the most advanced modern architecture is in some respects astonishing: they coincide with us in their reducing things to a human scale, in their asymmetric yet organic way of laying out the different levels, in how they managed to incorporate the gardens and landscape into the buildings themselves, in their strictly uncluttered use of materials and in so many other aspects which would be laborious to enumerate." And it is true, that the Alhambra, for all its great age, is in both its design and construction a very modern architectural concept.

The Swiss architect Le Corbusier found his view of modern architecture already defined in this monument as "the intelligent, just and magnificent interplay of volumes made harmonious by daylight ". He went on to express this as his ideal in his Cité Moderne (1922). They tried to bring the garden and the landscape into

View from the Comares Tower

Panoramic view from the Albaicín

their buildings and they always maintained their scale within human bounds.

Francisco Prieto Moreno, who was for many years the architect in charge of restoring and preserving the monument, said, "The Alhambra combines in its various buildings many architectural precepts which are still valid today, and are of course considered as masterpieces". Another great achievement in its construction is that although it was built over different periods and on a very uneven site the builders still managed to keep the axes and vertices of its courtyards symmetrical, thus imparting an overall impression of complete regularity and harmony.

And so it was: the Alhambra was not planned out entirely from the start; it grew outwards over the centuries from the original IX century fortress, the Alcazaba, gradually increasing in splendour as the years went by.

In the XIV century, during the reigns of the great builders, the sultans Yusuf I and his son Muhammad V, the Alhambra stood out like a blaze of white light against the terraced gardens of the Generalife silhouetted against the Hill of the Sun. But if the Alhambra was white, why is it called "the Red"?. The most widely known explanation is one originally offered by Yusuf's vizier, Ibn al-Khatib, who attributes the name to the colour of the light given off by the torches at night during the hurried construction of the surrounding ramparts. According to Ibn al-Khatib, to those living in the plain below the whole palace seemed to glow red in the dark and so they called it al-Hamra (the Red). We ought to bear in mind, however, that Ibn al-Khatib was

also one of the most renowned poets of his time and so we might do well to suspect that this account is a "poetic" version of the truth. More probably the name refers to the red colour of the soil of the hill itself and also includes a pun on the nickname of the first Nasrid emir "al-Hamar", or "the Red".

Titus Burckhardt comments, "The Alhambra was more than a palace, it was a complete city, albeit on a small scale, with its dwellings, administrative offices, garrisons, stables, mosques, schools, baths, cemeteries and gardens. Of all this there only remains the part corresponding to the royal palace itself. And it is almost a miracle that even this has survived, because despite its splendour it was built so insubstantially it almost seems that the builders didn't care. The fortifications as such are strong indeed - they had to be - but the buildings inside the city walls were not built to endure. This would reflect Moslem thought and their ideas about the transitory nature of things: the house of the king is only a temporary dwelling place. This is but one of the many contradictions that the Alhambra offers us if we look at it in the light of the rules concerning the construction of princely dwellings which we take for granted in the rest of Europe. But it is precisely in this "difference" that the hidden meaning of Granadan architecture lies. In contrast to all the royal residences in Christian Europe, the Alhambra has no façade; it has no main axis about which the buildings are disposed; the rooms are not aligned in such a way as to pass from one to another, from the prelude to the final apotheosis. Instead, at the ends of elusive corridors one finds oneself in hidden courtyards around which rooms are

grouped as though by chance. One might never suspect what other worlds may still be concealed behind the walls. It is somewhat like the oriental tale of a traveller who is thrown into a salt quarry and finds there an underground palace replete with orchards and maidens, where he lives happily for twelve years until one day he opens a secret little doorway which leads him into an even more magnificent palace." The same writer goes on to add, "Classical European architecture always tries to involve the observer in the interplay of static forces, and to this end the chief component is the pillar, resembling the human form and giving proportion to what rises above it and what rests upon it; the plinths, pillars, arches and entablature also accentuate these forces, all of which form an integral part of the construction.

Nothing of this sort can be seen in the Alhambra. Here, the smooth, weightless surfaces of the walls are perforated; the walls, windows and arches, which should manifest their own structural solidity, dissolve into subtle honeycombs, into shimmering light, and the columns in the arcaded rooms are so slim that the structure rising above them seems to be lighter than air. The architecture of the Alhambra doesn't permit the visitor to enter with dramatic mien; it doesn't magnify the experience of power beyond the human scale; it is completely indifferent, limpid and serene, like geometry, of which Plato says that no-one should enter into the mansion of wisdom without it." (T. Burckhardt)

View of the Alhambra from the orchards below the Generalife

PILAR DE CARLOS V

THE FOUNTAIN OF CHARLES V

THE CHARLES V FOUNTAIN REFLECTS THE DESIRE OF THE CONQUERORS OF ISLAM TO CHRISTIANISE THE NASRID CITY WITHOUT DETRACTING FROM ITS PAST GLORY AND TO EMPHASISE ITS IMPORTANCE AS THE NEW IMPERIAL CAPITAL. WITHIN THIS CONTEXT OF RESPECTING THE OLD WHILST AFFIRMING THE REALITY OF THE NEW, THIS MAGNIFICENT FOUNTAIN WAS PLACED AT THE ENTRANCE TO THE ALHAMBRA. IT WAS DESIGNED BY PEDRO MACHUCA AND SCULPTED BY NICCOLO DA CORTE IN 1543 TO FILL A NEW SPACE AND DEFINE A NEW ERA. IT IS NOT CERTAIN WHETHER THE MYSTERIOUS MASKS ARE MEANT TO REPRESENT GRANADA'S THREE RIVERS, THE GENIL, THE DARRO AND THE BEIRO, OR THREE SEASONS, SYMBOLISED IN THE VEGETAL ORNAMENTS: EARS OF WHEAT FOR SUMMER, FLOWERS FOR SPRING AND GRAPES FOR AUTUMN. WHATEVER THEIR INTENDED SIGNIFICANCE, THEY ARE LATER BAROQUE ADDITIONS TO THE FOUNTAIN. THE SHIELDS OF THE CITY OF GRANADA, THE TENDILLA FAMILY AND THE HAPSBURGS ARE REPEATED THROUGHOUT THE ORNAMENTATION OF THE FOUNTAIN, WHICH IS IN THE FINEST CLASSICAL STYLE.

PUERTA DE LA JUSTICIA

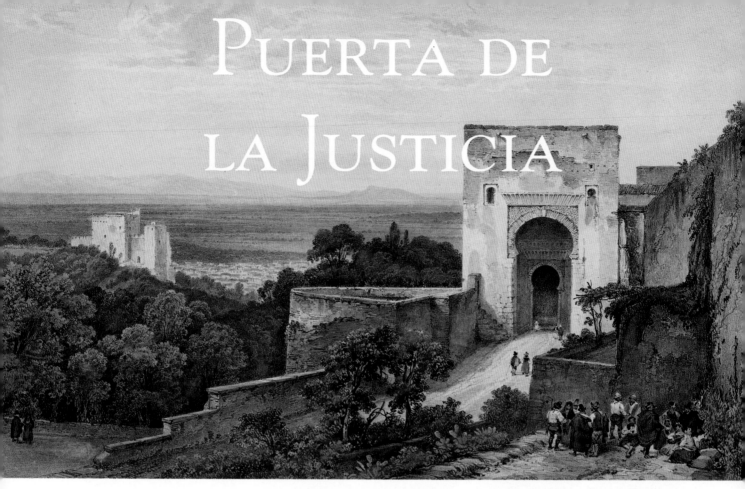

XIX century engraving of the Justice Gate

Charles V Fountain and the Justice Gate

THE GATE OF JUSTICE

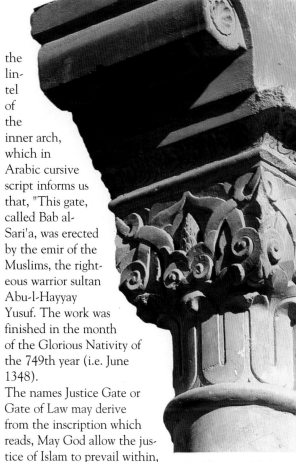

Du` `ring Muslim times the main entrance into the Madinat al-Hamra was by the Arms Gate to the north of the city, where any visitor would have had to pass along a strictly controlled route and be thoroughly inspected by the guard before arriving at the Watchtower. After the Christian reconquest, however, the whole fortress was adapted to suit new styles of military tactics and refurbished to suit Castillian taste. Perhaps one of the most important reforms was to change the orientation of life in the citadel to fit in with the new road leading to it, which we know today as the Cuesta de Gomérez, climbing up between the hills of the Alhambra and Mauror. The focus of attention was drawn away from the Arms Gate to the north and the main entrances became the Gate of Justice and the Wine Gate to the south.

The Gate of Justice is nowadays without doubt the most important gateway to the Citadel of the Alhambra. It stands imposingly at the top of a long slope in the shape of a projecting square tower with its rear edge butting against the city wall. Even today it retains its erstwhile majesty, in defiance of time, centuries of neglect and the fireworks which are let off inside it every Easter.

We know precisely when it was built from a panel above the lintel of the inner arch, which in Arabic cursive script informs us that, "This gate, called Bab al-Sari'a, was erected by the emir of the Muslims, the righteous warrior sultan Abu-l-Hayyay Yusuf. The work was finished in the month of the Glorious Nativity of the 749th year (i.e. June 1348).

The names Justice Gate or Gate of Law may derive from the inscription which reads, May God allow the justice of Islam to prevail within, although this could also refer to the city as a whole. It is sometimes called the Esplanade Gate because of the open esplanade that used to spread out in front of it before the two present-day roads were laid, one forking to the left towards the Generalife and the other through the woods to the right. Carved into the keystone of the outer arch there is a hand raised palm outwards, which has been subject to various interpretations. It may be a traditional sign of peace but it has also been plausibly proposed that it represents the five fingers referred to by Muslims as al-Hamza, the five basic precepts of Islam: a belief in one God and in his prophet Muhammad, to pray five times every day, to give alms, to fast during Ramadan and to go on a pilgrimage to Mecca at least once in one's lifetime. On the spandrel of the second, or inner arch, directly below the lintel and the panel explaining the origin of the gateway, there is a tasselled key, the significance of which is also open to debate. It may have been part of the arms of the Nasrid dynasty in Granada, as claimed by Hurtado de Mendoza, a Christian commander of the time, or else a general symbol of peace and welcome to the well-intentioned. (As far as this goes, keys are to be found adorning the lintels of mediaeval doorways in other parts of Europe.) Whatever it symbolises, the key is

Marble Capital belonging to the inner arch; in its day it would have been polychromed as would the rest of the doorway.

Upward slope inside the Justice Gate

Massive wooden door of the Justice Gate with its original iron bolt

repeated on the nearby Wine Gate and in the Dismounting Courtyard at the entrance to the Generalife. Above the panel is a niche containing a Gothic image of the Virgin Mary, although only a copy of the statue carved by Ruperto Alemán at the behest of the Catholic Monarchs, whose yoke-and-arrow emblems can be seen adorning the base.

Just inside the inner arch hang two massive iron-bound doors, with their original locks and bolts.

Between the outer arch, which, huge as it is was probably never closed by doors, and the inner arch, there is a confined defensive area, typical of Nasrid military building, where those defending the gate could hurl rocks, boiling oil or molten lead from the tower above onto any assailants trying to break down the door to the inner arch below them.

Beyond these arches the entrance continues to rise in the form of a ramp with four right-angled corners covered by squinched vaults with lunettes to provide light. This way of breaking up a straight run into the city is very much in character with the strategic nature of the gate; every corner provides a potential point of resistance. This feature is typical of Almohad military architecture throughout Andalucía. This ramp finally passes through a third, or innermost arch, into the confines of the citadel. On the spandrel of the horseshoe arch of this inner gate there are vestiges of beautiful blue and white enamelled rhomboid mosaics.

Once past the gate itself an enemy force's troubles would not be over; they would arrive at the *corraleta*, a wide passageway where horsemen would be arrayed waiting to

charge downhill against the uphill attack.

To the right of the gate there is a pathway which runs between the parapets around the entire city wall, sometimes covered, sometimes open to the sky, but always protected sufficiently to allow the guards to make their rounds on horseback.

The wall running along the left-hand side of the *corraleta* obviously collapsed at some time and was reconstructed with head-stones from a Muslim cemetery.

THE HORSESHOE ARCH

It is curious to learn that the form most readily associated with Islamic architecture, the horseshoe arch, was in fact introduced into Spain by the Visigoths. Witness, for example, the VI century church of San Juan de Baños in the Province of Palencia, where the Visigothic horseshoe arch predates the first Arab invasion by 50 years. Nevertheless the Arab invaders quickly adopted this style of arch and used it extensively with consummate skill (see the Grand Mosque in Córdoba, for example). Thus the horseshoe arch was exported from Spain throughout the Islamic world and became a symbol of Muslim architecture.

THE BLACK DEATH

It is ironic to note that 1348, the year this gateway was finished represented a period of wealth and promise for the Nasrid dynasty in their kingdom of Granada. It was also the year in which Bocaccio finished "The Decameron" . And it was the year in which the first epidemic of "black death" struck, killing possibly a third of the population of Europe in a few years.

Inside the Justice Gate

Las Fortificaciones

The Fortificacions

The Nasrid kingdom of Granada was constantly under threat of attack from its Christian adversaries lined along its borders to the north and west. Consequently almost every vantage point throughout its territory is dominated by a solid, square fortification, built of brick or rubble and lime mortar. Their accesses are typically narrow and staggered to make any direct assault as difficult as possible and the enemy would be subject to intense attack from wooden machicolations supported on corbels projecting from the walls.

ALCAZABA

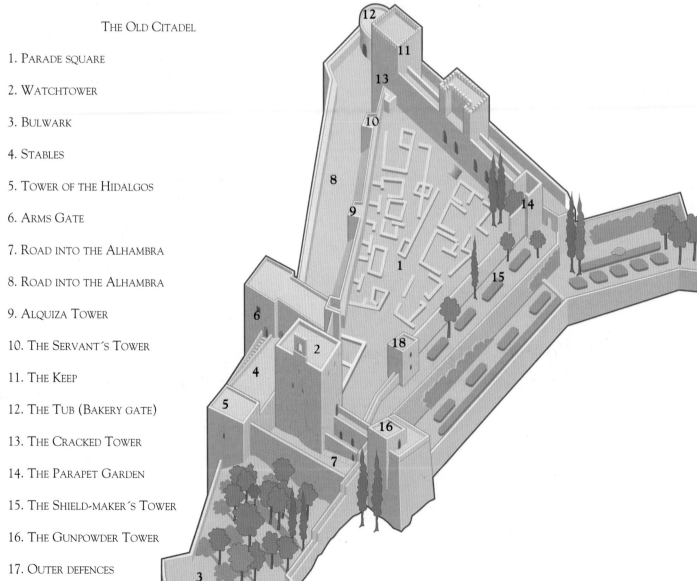

THE ALCAZABA (THE CITADEL)

The Alcazaba, unjustly forgotten by all those who after the Christian reconquest wrote in dazzling terms about the Nasrid palaces, is the solitary forbear of an entire aristocratic city, which would later come to be known as madinat al-Hamra (The citadel of the Alhambra). It is referred to in the accounts of the civil wars in the IX century and battles against the invading Almoravids and Almohads by various different names such as the fortress of Elvira or Granada Castle until, from the XIII century onwards, the name qa'lat al-Hamra (the red castle) becomes fixed and it is by this name that we know it today.

The Alcazaba comprises two clearly distinguishable precincts, one within the other. The smaller of the two, the inner ward (coloured brown) may well be Roman in origin, as might be deduced from the stone blocks in the footings of the walls (below). It is also known to have been rebuilt and strengthened during the caliphate of Abd ar-Rahman III to protect it from assault by the rebel Mozarabs and Muladis under the command of Umar ibn Hafsun.

For a long time, even after Muhammad ibn Nasr al-Ahmar arrived in Granada in 1238, the Alcazaba was an isolated fortress, separated by a deep gully from the plain to its east, where the royal palaces were later to be built.

During the reign of Yusuf 1 (1333 - 54) a long stretch of wall and towers were erected along the edge of this gully, some of the remains of which can still be seen in the Cistern Square close to the Wine Gate.

Yusuf also joined the walls of the Alcazaba to those of the royal palace by way of a parapet walkway along the battlements, which was reached via a stairway in the Bakery Tower, rediscovered in 1955 below the so-called Tub Tower.

In 1494, two years after the Christian conquest, the Count of Tendilla, had the gully filled in to make an *aljibe* or water cistern, using the Cracked Tower as a filter for the water. He covered the cistern with the square that still exists today in front of the Alcazaba. The summit of the Watchtower offers the visitor magnificent uninterrupted views all around.

TORRE DEL HOMENAGE (THE KEEP)

This is one of the oldest towers of the Alcazaba, probably dating back to the caliphate. Archaeological comparisons between the building materials of the actual tower and those in its foundations suggest that it may have been rebuilt by Muhammad I upon the ruins of a previous IX century structure.

PUERTA DE LAS ARMAS (THE ARMS GATE)

This gate used to be the main entrance to the Alcazaba. It butts onto the inner precinct of the Alcazaba as a flanking tower to the Torre de la Vela.

TORRE DE LA VELA (THE WATCHTOWER)

This tower was originally built by the founder of the Nasrid dynasty, Muhammad ibn Nasr al Ahmar (ruled 1238-73), as his feudal residence.

CUBO DE LA ALHAMBRA (THE TUB)

This round, squat tower houses the Puerta de la Tahona (The Bakery Gate), a XVI century renaissance addition after the Christian conquest.

TORRE QUEBRADA (THE CRACKED TOWER)

Known thus because of the great crack in its wall, stretching like a wound from top to bottom, which can be seen from the Plaza de los Aljibes. The tower has been filled in up to the height of the city wall but has two more floors above this level.

The Old Citadel (Alcazaba) seen from Comares Tower

Panoramic view eastward from the top of the Old Citadel towards the Generalife and the Hill of the Sun

PLAZA DE LAS ARMAS (THE PARADE GROUND)

Leading away from a cobbled slope at the top of this square there was a main street of shops and other civic buildings.

TORRE DE LA SULTANA (THE SULTANA'S TOWER)

As the photograph below shows, this tower rises majestically above the Parapet Garden. It must have lost some of its slender elegance when the deep walkway was filled in to make the garden.

JARDÍN DEL ADARVE (THE PARAPET GARDEN)

A deep walkway separated the outer and inner ramparts until the beginning of the XVII century, when it was filled in with rubble and earth by the Marquis of Mondéjar to make this garden.

TORRE DE LA PÓLVORA (THE GUNPOWDER TOWER)

From here a gateway spans the deep ravine of the Cuesta de Gomérez (known as *the moat of molten silver*). A path runs across the top of the gate, thus linking the Alcazaba to the Vermilion Towers on the other side. The later Christian additions: "the Tub", external wall and filled-in parapet walkway are coloured red.

The Bulwark, the true prow of the Alcazaba was added on by the Nasrids in the XV century as an emplacement for their artillery, facing, it should be noted, the city itself. It would appear that in the dynastic intrigues of the time the ruler of the day feared the inhabitants of the town below more than any possible foreign invader.

TORRE Y PUERTA DE LAS ARMAS
(THE ARMS TOWER AND GATE)

This was the main entrance to the outer bailey and was equipped with a portcullis controlled from the floor immediately above the gate, which could only be reached from the battlements of the Alcazaba.

Beyond the entrance a wide passageway turns sharply to the right, where there is a spacious room, obviously the guardroom. From here the way forks to the left towards the royal palaces and to the right to the Alcazaba.

On the way to the royal palaces any visitor or ambassador with his retinue, whether on foot or on horseback, had to cover a distance of some ninety yards with his unshielded right side exposed to archers stationed on the inner wall and on the parapet of the keep (right).

After passing another inspection in what is now the Tub (above) he would arrive at the market, the remains of which are still visible. In consonance with its popular name, this Christian tower is round and squat, making it less vulnerable to the artillery fire that was beginning to be used to great effect at this time.

For anyone wanting to visit the Alcazaba the approach was no easier. He had to leave his mount at the stables next door to the Arms Gate and then follow a path so narrow that two people could hardly walk abreast, up and down steps and around corners, for a distance of at least three times the width of the Watchtower. All this time he was under the scrutiny of the soldiers on the ramparts, who could stop a whole army if they wanted to just by throwing rocks, boiling oil or molten lead down onto the tortuous passageway running below them.

In the earliest extant painting of Granada, probably by the Flemish painter Petrus Cristus (ca. 1500), now in the Mateu collection (below), there is a door leading

into the Alcazaba which had been blocked up centuries ago. Through careful examination of the picture in 1894, Manuel Gómez Moreno was able to rediscover the door hidden within the wall. Within the inner precinct the foundations still remain of a bath-house for the soldiers at the foot of the watchtower and small houses along each side of a main street intended for officers of the garrison, armourers, blacksmiths and the such. There are also water cisterns, and a subterranean dungeon beneath the eastern wall, in which the prisoners' sleeping areas are laid out in brick.

TORRE DE LA VELA (THE WATCHTOWER)

The watchtower measures 16m by 16m and is 27m high. Its four floors underwent considerable transforma-

tion when they were converted into living quarters after the Christian conquest. The tower is not quite so high as it was originally, having lost its battlements in the various catastrophes that it has undergone since the XVI century: first an earthquake in 1522; then in 1590 a gunpowder factory exploded in the valley of the river Darro just below, leaving it considerably the worse for wear; and finally in 1882 the bell gable was struck by lightning. This has since been replaced, but in the centre of the west wall rather than in its original position at the north-west corner of the tower.

The views from the top of the Watchtower, as might be expected, encompass the whole of Granada and the surrounding countryside as far as the eye can see.

GRANADA'S CITY WALLS

GRANADA'S FORTIFICATIONS HAVE GROWN IN CONSONANCE WITH THE CITY ITSELF. THE OLDEST STILL PRESERVED IS THAT OF THE X CENTURY ALCAZABA CADIMA IN THE ALBAICÍN, FROM THE ZIRID DYNASTY, ALTHOUGH THERE ARE REMAINS OF OTHERS BUILT UPON EARLIER STRUCTURES DATING FROM ROMAN AND EVEN IBERIAN TIMES.

THE ALHAMBRA REPRESENTED A KEY ELEMENT IN A COMPLEX SYSTEM OF WALLS SURROUNDING THE CITY OF GRANADA, ALTHOUGH ITS POSITION IS SOMEWHAT CURIOUS IN THAT IT REALLY REMAINED OUTSIDE THE MAIN BODY OF THE TOWN, AS THOUGH FEARING THE INHABITANTS OF GRANADA MORE THAN ENEMIES FROM AFAR. IN FACT, WHEN MUHAMMAD IBN NASR AL-AHMAR FOUNDED HIS DYNASTY IN GRANADA HE FIRST OCCUPIED THE ALCAZABA CADIMA ON THE ALBAICÍN, WHICH WAS AFTER ALL THE CITY AT THAT TIME, THE RED HILL BEING TO ALL INTENTS AND PURPOSES UNINHABITED. BUT WHEN THE NEW RESIDENTIAL QUARTERS THAT QUICKLY GREW UP AROUND HIS FORTRESS BEGAN TO BLOCK AN EASY WAY OF RETREAT, HE DECIDED IT WOULD BE MORE PRUDENT TO RESTORE THE CITADEL ON THE HILL ON THE OTHER SIDE OF THE RIVER DARRO, WHICH, ALTHOUGH NEEDING CONSIDERABLE REPAIR, OFFERED HIM OPEN TERRAIN IF HE EVER NEEDED TO FLEE IN A HURRY.

IN THE XII CENTURY WHAT IS NOW THE CENTRE OF GRANADA HAD BEEN BROUGHT WITHIN THE CITY WALLS AND DURING THE NASRID DYNASTY THE HIGHER DISTRICTS OF THE ALBAICÍN AND, MORE IMPORTANTLY, GARNATA AL-YEHUD, THE JEWISH QUARTER, WHICH LIES JUST BELOW THE ALHAMBRA ON THE MAUROR HILL, WERE ALSO ENCLOSED. IT IS OF COURSE FROM THE GARNATA (VILLAGE OF THE FOREIGNERS) OF THIS DISTRICT THAT THE MODERN NAME OF THE CITY, GRANADA, DERIVES. ENTRANCE COULD BE GAINED INTO THE ENLARGED MEDIAEVAL CITY OF GRANADA THROUGH NUMEROUS GATES, OF WHICH THOSE REMAINING *IN SITU* ARE THE GATES OF ELVIRA, MONAITA, ARCO DE LAS PESAS, HIZNA ROMAN AND FAJALAUZA, ALL IN THE AREA OF THE ALBAICÍN. A FEW OTHERS HAVE BEEN MOVED FROM THEIR ORIGINAL POSITIONS AND REBUILT ELSEWHERE.

Squally sunset over the Alhambra seen from the Albaicín

PUERTA
DEL VINO

THE WINE GATE

IT IS GENERALLY ACCEPTED THAT THE NAME OF THIS GATE DERIVES FROM THE TAX-FREE WINE THAT WAS SOLD INSIDE THE PORTAL FROM 1554. THERE WERE OTHER GATES NEARBY BUT WITHIN THE INTRICATE LABYRINTH OF THE MEDIAEVAL CITY THIS WAS THE GATE WHICH GAVE MOST DIRECT ACCESS TO THE HIGHER REACHES OF THE CITY, HOME TO SOME 2,000 INHABITANTS. AT THIS POINT THE ROYAL WAY, THE MAIN ARTERY OF THE *MEDINA* BEGAN; IT WAS ALSO A CROSSROADS AND THE DIVIDING LINE BETWEEN THE MILITARY AND CIVIL AREAS OF THE TOWN.

THE **EASTERN FAÇADE** IS THE MOST INTERESTING AND ORNAMENTAL. IT CONTAINS FINE, CERAMIC TILING, PAINTED AND FIRED USING THE DRY-CORD TECHNIQUE, ELABORATE DECORATIVE GESSO AND VESTIGES OF STUCCO-WORK WITH HINTS OF POLYCHROMING, WHICH MUST AT ONE TIME HAVE COVERED MANY OF THE WALLS OF THE ALHAMBRA. THE **WESTERN FAÇADE** IS OLDER AND MORE ROUGHLY EXECUTED. THE GATEWAY ITSELF HAS ONE OF THE FEW STILL EXTANT POINTED HORSESHOE ARCHES. IT IS ALSO EMBLAZONED WITH THE MYSTERIOUS SYMBOLIC KEY

El Mexuar

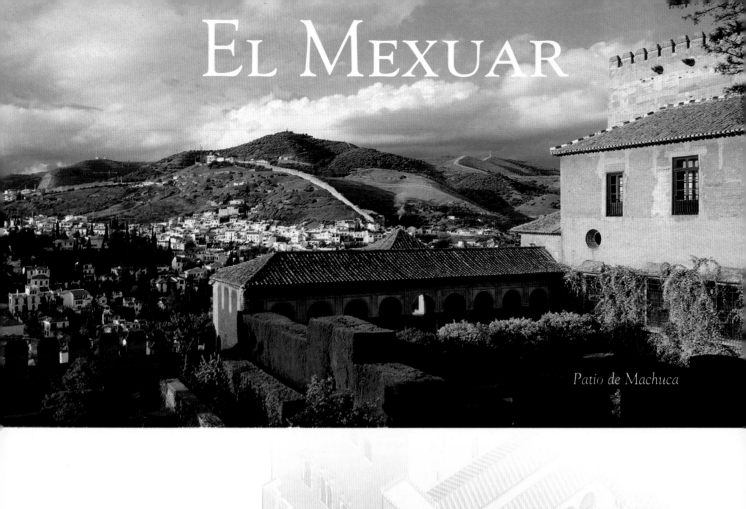

Patio de Machuca

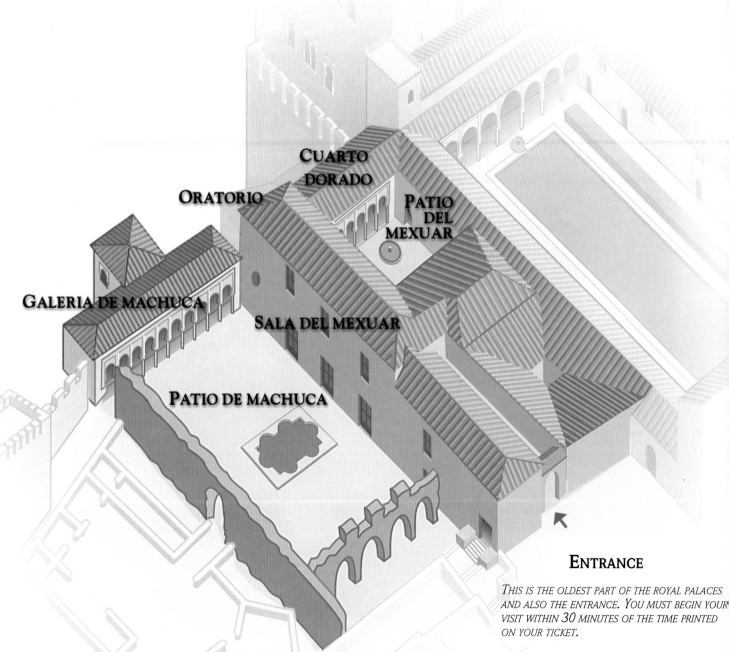

CUARTO DORADO

ORATORIO

PATIO DEL MEXUAR

GALERIA DE MACHUCA

SALA DEL MEXUAR

PATIO DE MACHUCA

ENTRANCE

THIS IS THE OLDEST PART OF THE ROYAL PALACES AND ALSO THE ENTRANCE. YOU MUST BEGIN YOUR VISIT WITHIN 30 MINUTES OF THE TIME PRINTED ON YOUR TICKET.

THE OLD ROYAL HOUSE

The Hall or Room of the Mexuar

Not long after the Christian conquest the Nasrid palaces were referred to as the Old Royal House in order to distinguish them from the New Royal House, the palace that Charles V intended to build as the great residential, administrative and political centre of the new Spanish empire. This distinction implied a clear intention to integrate the Nasrid buildings into the projected scheme of the new Alhambra. The Catholic monarchs had no fixed residence and so when their grandson, Charles I of Spain, later the emperor Charles V, chose the Alhambra as the site of his own palace he unwittingly saved it for posterity. The Old Royal House comprises today, as it did then, the most important focal points of the Alhambra: the Mexuar (council chamber) and the two palaces of Comares and the Lions, together with their annexes and outbuildings, all of which merit individual explanation within the context of the palace complex as a whole. References have been made to seven palaces within the citadel and there is no doubt that only a small part of the

original royal town and some vestiges of the *medina* remain today, but sufficient to give us some idea of the splendour and majesty of a civilisation at its cultural height, although politically in decline.

The Alhambra has justly been declared a monument of human heritage. Beyond the purely architectural it is a creation of space, air and light. But it is not a space filled within a void; it is rather a captured amalgam of brightness and shadow, streams and flowers, enveloped in verse and sensations which transcend time.

Machuca's Courtyard is named after the famous architect Pedro Machuca, who designed the Palace of Charles V and lived in the tower with an arched portico on the north side of the courtyard overlooking the river Darro. On the opposite side of the courtyard there was an identical gallery, of which only vestiges remain in the ground, but an idea of its layout and form can still be seen in the arches of cypress trees growing where it used to be.

The Mexuar is without doubt the area of the palace complex that has undergone most transformation since its earliest days, changes which were largely made by the Christian governors in the name of their king to adapt it to new roles and functions. Thus its original shape has been altered considerably, sometimes to the detriment of earlier structures, and so it is quite difficult nowadays to

The hall of the Mexuar

establish exactly where the entrances to this part of the palace really were.

THE HALL OF THE MEXUAR is almost certainly the oldest surviving part of the royal palaces but it has undergone substantial alterations, either during the reign of Yusuf 1 or of his son Muhammad V. It was here that the royal court of justice is believed to have convened. After the conquest the Christian monarchs installed their chapel here, changing the shape of the room once again. A hypothetical reconstruction of its original appearance can be seen below.

The small door guarding the entrance today is a later introduction brought from elsewhere. It has fine carved surrounds and is sheltered by overhanging eaves supported by elegant corbels.

The original hall was illuminated by daylight filtering through the stained-glass panes of a lantern window in the roof. This was later replaced by an artistically carved, radial, wooden ceiling.

An original wall at the northern end of the hall, which closed it off from either a small yard or a street, was demolished to amplify the hall. The decorative gesso covering the original wall was saved and used on the new wall, which contains a doorway leading to the erstwhile oratory, later used as a sacristy.

The present-day wooden balustrade represents the remains of a choir, which was added in the space gained when the exterior yard was included within the hall.

The eastern wall was reinforced to support the weight of a new floor added above the hall. Great windows with wrought-iron grilles were opened up to give more light to the room. It is impossible to determine what the surface of this wall might originally have looked like.

The council met within the square formed by the four columns to decide upon important judicial matters. At the door there was a tile which reads,

Enter and ask. Do not be afraid to seek justice for here you will find it.

The whole room, including the part belonging to the yard, which was included into the Mexuar proper in Christian times, has a dado of XVI century Morisco tiling. In the central stars the arms of the Nasrid dynasty alternate with those of Cardinal Mendoza, the double-headed eagle of the House of Austria and the Pillars of Hercules from the imperial shield, all of which suggests an admiration on the part of the Christians for things Muslim and a certain desire to integrate the two cultures. The present entrance was opened in modern times, dis-

The Tower of the Dagger, Machiuca's Courtyard, Comares Tower and the Albaicín district to the left.

The Mexuar Oratory

turbing one of the XVI century tiles showing the Pillars of Hercules, which was moved to a position on the east wall, although the gypsum crown above it remains in its original position above the new doorway.

THE MEXUAR ORATORY

The oratory is situated at the end of the main hall overlooking the Albaicín. It is one of the rooms that suffered most damage from the explosion of the gunpowder factory in the valley below in 1590. Repairs were begun at once but it was not completely restored until 1917. In Nasrid times entrance to the oratory was by way of the Machuca gallery.

Along the northern wall are four arched windows, three of which have marble-pillar mullions with alabaster capitals.

The restoration work bears little in common with the original decoration and so the visitor need pay scant attention to the simplified mural adornments, with the exception perhaps of some epigraphs around the *mihrab*, relating to Muhammad V, and one which says,

> *Do not be negligent: come to prayer.*

Islam obliges the faithful to pray towards Mecca five times a day and so oratories of this sort are to be found everywhere throughout Muslim countries. Their main feature is the decorated devotional niche, the mihrab, which indicates the direction towards Mecca.

It can be seen that the orientation of this small oratory does not conform to the line of the battlements but slants to the south east in the direction of Mecca.

THE COURTYARD OF THE MEXUAR

This small courtyard used to be called, for no good reason, the Courtyard of the Mosque. On its southern side is an impressive façade, always accepted as having been the entrance to the Comares Palace. Opposite, on the northern side, with a portico in front of it, is the so-called Golden Chamber

Engravings of this patio from centuries past should be evidence enough to exonerate later restorers from any feelings of blame we might bear towards them; as far as this courtyard is concerned, the extensive restoration work has been well carried out.

The eastern wall of the courtyard houses the entrance to a long tunnel, which leads eventually to the Comares Palace bath-

The Mexuar Courtyard and the Golden Chamber

house after passing small rooms on either side that must have served as soldiers' quarters or guard rooms.

The centre of the courtyard is occupied by a fountain with a fluted trough of white marble, although only a copy of the original. The gallery at the entrance to the Golden Chamber is composed of three arches resting upon what may be Almohad white-marble capitals, crowning slender marble columns. The two capitals with "handles" could well be a stylised interpretation of similar zoomorphic capitals to be found in Persepolis .

Coffered ceiling in the Golden Chamber

THE GOLDEN CHAMBER

Behind the gallery lies the Golden Chamber. Here a gothic window looks out across the woodlands beyond. The mullion of this window has a capital bearing the emblems of the Catholic monarchs.

It has been suggested that in Nasrid times this was where visitors waited to be admitted to the sultan's presence in the palace beyond. The original ceiling, fastened onto a hipped roof (see below), was restored during the reign of the Catholic Monarchs, who included Gothic motifs and copious gilt-work in the decoration, whence the name of the chamber.

THE FAÇADE OF COMARES

This façade of the Comares Palace was considerably restored in the XIX century. The entrance is raised above the level of the courtyard upon a plinth of three white marble steps. Its *ataurique* (foliate and vegetal) decoration becomes more intricate as it goes upwards, possibly in imitation of the ascending order of classical design.

The façade to this palace, at least in the form in which we know it today, was made to commemorate the successful siege of Algeciras by Muhammad V in 1369. The inscription quoted here would seem to refer to its unusual construction with two doors

The overhanging wooden eaves are supported by wooden corbels and a frieze. Their fine, elaborate carving is generally considered to represent the apotheosis of Spanish-Muslim carpentry.

According to some expert commentators on the subject this beautiful façade is not in its original position. Thus Oleg Grabar states, *It is too big and elaborate to be a simple doorway; looking at the overall composition the façade is out of balance with the tiny courtyard which precedes it and lacks any clear visual role; although the inscriptions do emphasise its pivotal position within the internal organisation of the palace.*

MUDEJAR WOODEN ROOF FRAMEWORKS
CARPENTRY ATTAINED NEW HEIGHTS OF MAGNIFICENCE IN ANDALUSIA IN ELEGANTLY CARVED WOODEN CEILINGS, WHICH, LIKE THE STUCCOED AND TILED WALLS OF THE ROOMS THEY COVERED, COMBINED PRACTICALITY WITH ARTISTIC AND SYMBOLIC BEAUTY.

MANY OF THE BUILDING TECHNIQUES OF AL-ANDALUS WERE KEPT UP BY SKILLED MOORISH CRAFTSMEN WHO CHOSE TO STAY IN SPAIN AFTER THEIR LANDS HAD BEEN CONQUERED BY THE CHRISTIANS. THEY WERE KNOWN AS MUDEJARS (FROM THE ARABIC *MUDAJJAN*, MEANING "PERMITTED TO REMAIN") AND WERE RESPONSIBLE FOR THE CONSTRUCTION OF MANY OF THE NEW BUILDING PROJECTS EMBARKED ON IN THE RECENTLY CONQUERED CITIES, AMONG WHICH WERE THE CHURCHES ERECTED IN THE NAME OF THE NEW FAITH. IN THIS WAY THE TERM MUDEJAR CAME TO REPRESENT AN ARCHITECTURAL STYLE IN ITS OWN RIGHT.

LA FACHADA DE COMARES

FAÇADE OF THE COMARES PALACE

"MY POSITION IS THAT OF A CROWN AND MY DOOR IS A PARTING OF THE WAYS: THE WEST BELIEVES THAT IN ME IS THE EAST. AL-GANI BI-LLAH HAS ENTRUSTED ME TO OPEN THE WAY TO THE VICTORY THAT HAS BEEN FORETOLD AND I AWAIT HIS COMING JUST AS THE HORIZON USHERS IN THE DAWN. MAY GOD ADORN HIS WORKS WITH THE SAME BEAUTY THAT RESIDES IN HIS COUNTENANCE AND HIS NATURE.

(INSCRIPTION WITHIN THE FRIEZE ON THE FAÇADE)

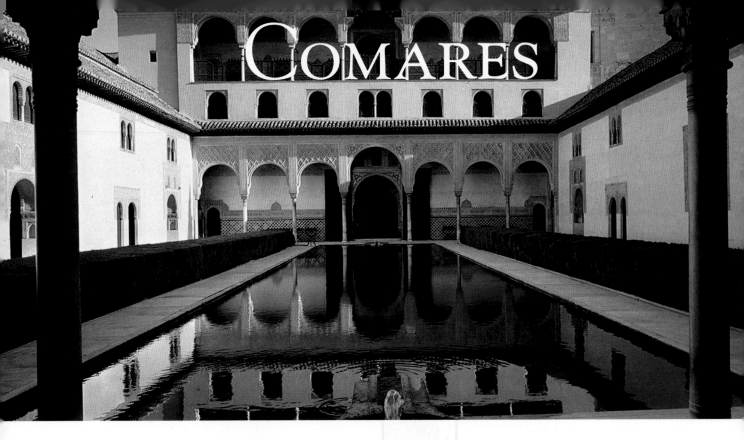

COMARES

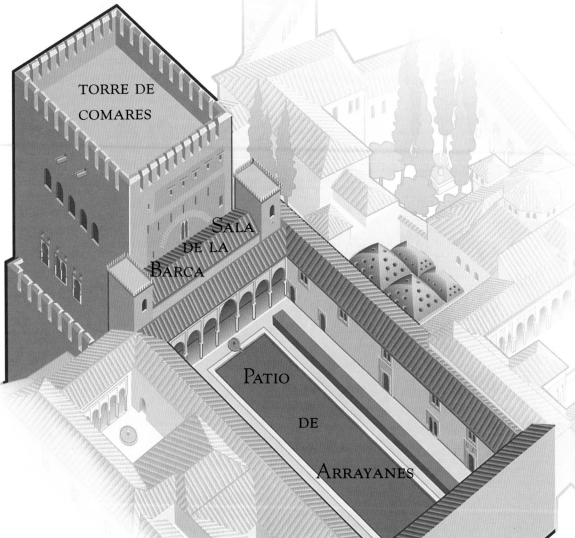

SALÓN

DEL

TRONO

TORRE DE

COMARES

SALA

DE LA

BARCA

PATIO

DE

ARRAYANES

THE COURTYARD OF THE MYRTLES

This was the focal point of diplomatic and political activity in the Alhambra and without doubt the place where great receptions for ambassadors were held. It was also where important visitors waited to be received by the sultan. Until recently the whole of this part of the building had been accredited to Yusuf I, apart from some of the decorative work corresponding to his son Muhammad V, to whom there is a panegyric in the wall of the north gallery, but a study by Emilio García Gómez has shown fairly convincingly that Yusuf I (1333-54) built the gallery and Hall of the Boat, the Comares Tower and the baths, whilst the rest was built during the reign of his son Muhammad V (1354-91).

The myrtle (*myrtus communis*) was frequently found in the gardens of al-Andalus. This courtyard owes its name to the myrtle bushes that border the central pool. They are evergreen and give off a very pleasant smell when their leaves are brushed or rubbed in the hand.

" ...when the rest of Europe was building castles in the air, in Granada they were constructing palaces upon water." (Jesús Bermúdez)

When a visitor crossed the main threshold he was confronted by a vast mirror of water reflecting the solid white bulk of the Comares Tower. The slope of the white marble floors allows the water in the pool to reach right up to the plinths of the columns on the north side of the courtyard and so the whole palace, even the tower itself, seems to be floating on water. This use of water to mirror the structure above was used some three centuries later (1630-47) in the Taj Mahal at Agra in India.

Water is the secret of the mysterious life of the Alhambra: it makes the gardens grow exuberantly green, it gives birth to the splendour of the flowering shrubs and bushes, it rests in the pools reflecting the elegantly arcaded halls, it dances in the fountains and murmurs in channels through the very heart of the royal palaces, just as the Koran describes Paradise as an orchard flowing with streams.

There has been some debate as to whether the skirting

Niche adorned with mocarab "stalactite plasterwork" in the Courtyard of the Myrtles

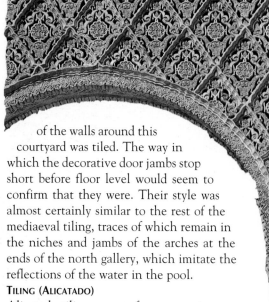

of the walls around this courtyard was tiled. The way in which the decorative door jambs stop short before floor level would seem to confirm that they were. Their style was almost certainly similar to the rest of the mediaeval tiling, traces of which remain in the niches and jambs of the arches at the ends of the north gallery, which imitate the reflections of the water in the pool.

TILING (ALICATADO)

Alicatado tiling, a sort of marquetry in stone, derives its name from the type of pincers, *al-qata'a,* or "alicate" in modern Spanish, used to trim the edges of the tiny ceramic pieces which it is composed of. These were put together on a flat surface like a jigsaw puzzle, but face downwards, and then covered in gypsum plaster. When the composition was dry it was cleaned and smoothed off before being put into place on the wall. When the pieces formed part of a repetitive pattern they were probably moulded and their edges clipped clean with pincers and sanded smooth. Alicatado tiling in the true sense of the word, however, was the technique of taking a simple piece of fired ceramic and shaping it with the pincers and a fine chisel. Although this craft has fallen into disuse in Spain it continues to this day in Morocco, where

craftsmen have inherited the artistic skills once common to al-Andalus and northern Africa. The process of making ceramics begins with collecting the clay: in Granada this probably came from the banks of the river Beiro. Afterwards it has to be mashed, suspended in water, filtered off and then trodden and kneaded into the shape required. Colours were obtained for mosaic tiling by melting siliceous sands, lead sulphide and other mineral-bearing ores in ovens and pounding them to obtain a fine powder, which, when mixed with water and other dyes, were painted onto the tiles before being baked.

The ceramics were baked in ovens divided into three sections: firebox, baking chamber and outer heat chamber. Using bushes and shrubs such as gorse for fuel, temperatures of up to 900 degrees could be reached. The baking process consisted of 24 hours' heating plus a similar period for slow cooling, two days and nights in all.

Virtuosity and refinement in the art of tiling is to be seen in the pillars in the Throne Room, where the tiles are moulded to the curvature of the columns).One of the most important aspects of the alicatado tiling is visual symmetry in one, two, three, four or even six axes and the way in which

Mosaic in the throne alcove

The Courtyard of the Myrtles at night

the smallest elements combine to form others of a higher dimension, such as this example from a jamb in the Lindaraja Tower, which includes three increasing dimensions of stars, each including the smaller dimension within itself. These repetitive rhythms can be extended to infinity and fill vast surfaces. The Alhambra is a veritable museum of ribbons of ingenious tracery.

The courtyard was an open esplanade during the reign of Yusuf I. His son, Muhammad V, built the gallery to enclose its southern end and thus make a private courtyard similar to the Greek *megaton* and Roman *atrium*, but having evolved here through the centuries to a design of sublime simplicity.

The solid cornice of the Palace of Charles V intrudes upon the delicate, insubstantial lines of the Courtyard of the Myrtles, bearing witness to two completely different ways of understanding shape and space.

The central arch of this gallery is higher than those beside it and rests upon *muqarna* capitals similar to those at Ispahan (left). The three other arches on each side rest upon square capitals. Most of the inscriptions in gesso and wood in the south portico are in praise of God and, apart from those dedicated to the sultan, are mainly copies from the

north side of the courtyard. The intrados of the arch behind the portico is covered in intricate leaf motifs in delicate shades of blue. Above the arch there are three windows with gypsum jalousies.

The two long walls along each side of the courtyard contain five doorways opening into small rooms. All these rooms have two floors, the upper one receiving daylight through arched windows, but it is not clear what these rooms were used for. The presence of brick daises on the floors of some of the rooms has led authors to claim that they were set aside for the women of the palace. Nevertheless, functionaries at this time also used to work sitting on such daises and they may have been used for administrative purposes.

THE NORTH GALLERY.is very similar to that on the south side and many of the decorative elements and epigraphs found in the south gallery were copied from this one. Above the XVI century tiled dado is a poem by Ibn Zamrak written in cursive script, which refers in one of its verses to the heroic deeds of Muhammad V:

"You conquered Algeciras with the might of your sword, opening a secret doorway to our victory."

The tree of life crowns the line of epigraphic verses

written around the wall. This type of design, in which *ataurique* plant motifs spread downwards from an apex is an allusion to the inverted tree that supports the celestial bodies in the firmament and buries its roots in paradise.

The coffered ceiling of this gallery was destroyed in a fire in 1890 along with that of the Sala de la Barca beside it. It has been very skilfully repaired, however, making use of many of the burnt pieces.

LA SALA DE LA BARCA (THE HALL OF THE BOAT)

This long room lies behind the gallery and serves as an anteroom to the Throne Room. At each end it has two alcoves framed by stilted arches and there is also a water closet on the west side. The roof of this hall, the restoration of which was completed in 1965, is a worthy reconstruction of the carved wooden, barrel-vaulted ceiling destroyed in the fire of 1890. The original was supported by a wooden framework in five sections. The greeting *baraka*, a blessing on you, appears everywhere among the inscriptions on the walls and it has been suggested that the name of the hall, barca or boat, may well derive from the phonetic mutation of this oft repeated word. Nevertheless, its ceiling in the shape of an upturned boat might have provided added visual support for the term. The muted tones of the ceramic tiles in the wainscot dates the construction of this hall to the first half of the XIV century.

Remains of polychroming are visible on the entrance arch (left) just as they are on the arch which leads into the Hall of Ambassadors. The large slabs of marble adorning the bottom of the entrance arches were poly-

Detail of the entrance to the Hall of the Ambassadors,

The Courtyard of the Myrtles

Espejismos

Ever-Shifting Images

If God is the Eternal One, so all of creation is but a part of the whole: fragile, mortal, deceptive. This concept of the elusiveness of reality and its constant flux became almost an obsession both because of its religious significance and in the effects it had upon artistic creations of the time, to the extent that an architect would construct only half of what was to be seen: the reflection of what was before him, a transient lightness, reality's other face. The tangible has no greater substance than its reflected image, although the latter may be an optical illusion. In the desert the horizon also seems to be continuously shifting, forming unattainable mirages.

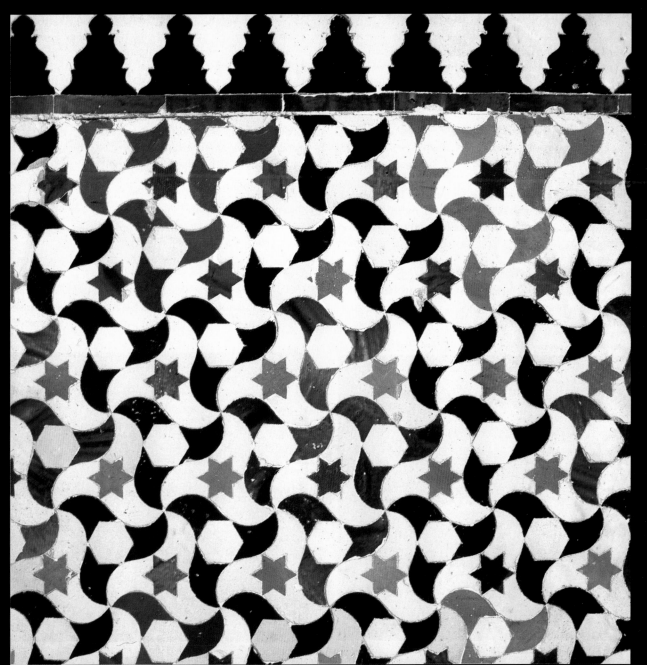

chromed in blue and gold and in places decorated with highly stylised deer similar to those painted on the amphora on show in the Alhambra Museum (left). One very well preserved example of these marble jambs is kept in the National Archaeological Museum. The small, beautifully sculpted marble or gesso niches in the jambs of the arches were for keeping jars of water, perfume or vases of flowers, but almost always water as a symbol of hospitality, according to the verses written around them.

THE HALL OF AMBASSADORS

This is the symbolic centre of Nasrid power; in it is concentrated the magnificence of the last Muslim court in Europe. Everything here speaks of splendour and refinement, from the gold leaf which can still be made out on the entrance arch and the intricate mosaic tiles to the magnificent ceiling covering the entire hall.

The overall plan of the Tower of Comares reveals the deceptive nature of its design; at 45 metres high it would appear to be a military tower, but the three deep alcoves in the walls on three sides would have greatly weakened its defensive capacity and reveal it for what it really was: a palatial reception hall. The alcoves themselves are covered with elegantly carved wooden ceilings. The five windows in each wall of the tower are reminiscent of desert architecture.

THE THRONE ROOM, OR HALL OF AMBASSADORS, is also called the Hall of Comares, deriving from the Arabic, *qamariyya*, meaning "stained glass". The alcoves, swimming in colours pouring through the stained glass windows, were favourite places for dignitaries and important visitors, who, just as in a desert tent, would always sit in the corners of a room.

The colours of the tiles in the wainscoting are extremely vivid whilst being perfectly balanced, although they lack the red which shone through the stained glass. According to the inscriptions that run along the wall above the tiling in the alcove itself, the central alcove on the north side of the hall was reserved for the throne: *Yusuf chose me to be the throne of the kingdom. May the Lord of the divine throne aid him in his grandeur.*

From here the sultan would have had a certain psychological advantage over his subjects, who would have felt themselves at one and the same time under the commanding but protective gaze of the political, military and religious leader of their kingdom. Foreign ambassadors too, as they crossed the threshold of the Sala de la Barca and walked towards the throne room, surrounded by brilliant colours and gleaming gold, would have felt intimidated by the scrutiny of the sultan, silhouetted against the more mysterious light of the stained glass behind him. The sultan himself, lying on his throne, could enjoy the view of Granada and its elegant houses and gardens, the sky and water, which was offered to his eyes as in a mirror in the Courtyard of the Myrtles.

The stained-glass windows of the throne room were destroyed by the explosion of a gunpowder factory in 1590. The geometric design of these windows was a transparent continuation of the tiled dado. In the windows, the fine straight lines that criss-cross the ceramics

The ceiling in its present condition

The ceiling in all the glory of its original colours, according to D. Darío Cabanelas

were represented by thin strips of lead holding each coloured pane in place. The light thus filtered through these coloured panes fell upon a blue and gold tiled floor, some vestiges of which remain, roped off in the centre of the hall.

The originals are those tiles in which the blues surrounding the dynastic shields are painted right to the edge and are completely flat, so as to be smooth for unshod feet. The later, post-conquest imitations stick up slightly around the edges of the colours.

The roof of the throne room is the culmination of Nasrid carpentry. It is composed of 8,017 separate pieces of wood in seven concentric circles with superimposed cedar-wood adornments and crowned in the centre with a sumptuous *muqarna* boss. The ribbon-work stars of both eight and sixteen formal elements were drawn according to the precise rules of a strict mathematical code. Nevertheless, Gómez Moreno inclines to the belief that their drawing can be put down more to the skill of artisans using compasses and set squares than to numerical calculation.

The *muqarna* boss represents paradise. Its heart is pure white, in comparison to all the rest of the centres of the stars, which are light walnut, an imperfect reflection of divinity. The walls are veritable tapestries of delightful stucco motifs and epigraphs which border on perfection.

The inscriptions in Kufic script and Maghrib and Andalusian cursive characters recite mainly religious themes and praise to the sultan Yusuf I. Oft repeated is the oration,

The only conqueror is God.

An almost imperceptible inscription upon the capital of one of the arches to an alcove confirms the public nature of this hall: *Be brief and you will leave in peace.*

ARABESQUE: The artistic intention of the rhythmic repetition of the arabesque design is very different from that of figurative art, it might almost be said to be the contrary; it doesn't try to imprison the gaze and direct it to some imaginary world but rather frees it from all the impediments of thought and imagination, in the same way as when we look at running water, the wind blowing a field of wheat, falling snowflakes or flames flickering up the chimney. It produces in us no fixed idea, just an existential condition, a feeling of tranquility combined with an inner sense of vitality.

The Hall of Ambassadors

37

El Patio de los Leones

THE COURTYARD OF THE LIONS

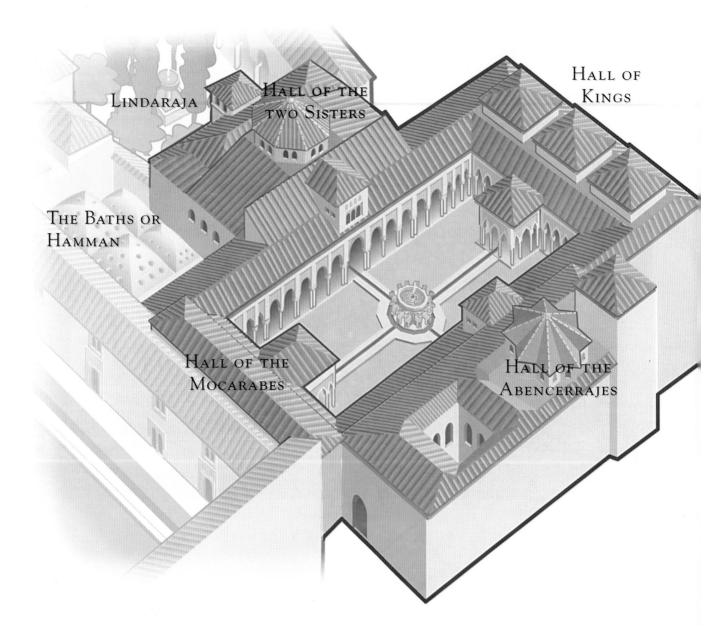

LINDARAJA

HALL OF THE TWO SISTERS

HALL OF KINGS

THE BATHS OR HAMMAN

HALL OF THE MOCARABES

HALL OF THE ABENCERRAJES

THE COURTYARD OF THE LIONS

his was the focal point of the sultan's private dwellings, within which there were areas set aside for the women of the house. It cannot be called the harem because it wasn't reserved exclusively for female use but was also probably used for some aspects of the sultan's political and diplomatic affairs. It is recorded that on December 30 1362, during the second reign of Mohammad V, nothing more existed of the Courtyard of the Lions than the Sala de las Dos Hermanas (The Hall of the two Sisters) and so the buildings that surround it today must have been constructed after this date.

From the original entrance, (lower corner of the plan on the facing page), the beauty of this patio progressively revealed itself to the visitor in either direction that he chose to take around the cloister. He found himself walking through a forest of gilded pillars, which little by little began to appear like "gold fringes of lace hanging from the sky".

The overhanging carved wooden eaves with beautifully sculpted corbels, which were originally polychromed, protected the adornments of the arches and columns below. The Nasrid motto, "The only conqueror is God" is repeated throughout the epigraphic surround. The columns are crowned by pilasters, which in turn hold up lintels supporting the upper structure of the walls. The gaps between the pilasters are filled by small, purely decorative, open-work, or "curtain" arches. The cubic capitals were originally polychromed. Their apparent uniformity is deceptive as their decoration is quite varied, which may not be obvious at first glance. The joints between the jambs of the columns and their capitals and plinths are made of lead to ensure that all three parts are perfectly seated and also to allow for expansion and contraction. "The integrity of Granadan art can be seen in the saturation of many single forms, such as the capitals on the columns in the Courtyard of the Lions. Never since the Egyptian lotus capitals have columns been crowned more elegantly, if by elegance we

Intrados in the Lindaraja Mirador

Reflection of the columns upon wet marble

understand simplicity combined with the finest degree of development of the artistic forms." (Oleg Grabar).

There has been interminable discussion about the original appearance of this courtyard, with decisions appealing to all tastes. An inscription in the Hall of the Two Sisters asks, "Have you ever seen such a beautiful garden?". "We have never seen a garden with greater abundance of fruit, nor sweeter nor more perfumed..."

But today its flowers no longer carpet the ground, nor do they climb and twine around the marble columns; what we see before us is no more than a magnificent skeleton, a dry empty framework to which greenery once gave meaning and life. To get an idea of the original appearance of this court-

Space in the Alhambra is as open as it is in the desert, where intimacy itself is to be found beneath the stars. The Courtyard of the Lions is not a house with a garden but a garden containing a house, which should be looked at from its corners at floor height; thus the photograph above, which complies more accurately with the point of view of its builders.

yard a visitor must have some understanding of the symbolic points of reference of its designers. Thus, from certain angles the forest of columns reminds us of the palm trees surrounding an oasis.

"According to Islamic tradition, the *hortus conclusus* or

walled garden is an image of paradise, the name of which in the Koran is *al-Yanna*, a word which embraces the two meanings of "garden" and "secret place". A visitor today must allow his imagination to see the four areas between the streams, which are today covered with sand, as beds full of flowering bushes and aromatic herbs. The four streams symbolise the four rivers of paradise that run towards the four points of the compass, or flow from them towards the centre" (Rafael Manzano).

Refreshing water springs from the mouths of twelve white marble lions in the Fountain of the Lions in the middle of the courtyard. Standing in a circle and bearing on their backs a twelve-sided bowl, they embrace every part of the courtyard in their gaze. Some experts say that at one time the whole fountain was polychromed, and indeed there is evidence to suggest that the lions have been scraped at some time in their lives. It is also believed that the lions may originally have come from a palace belonging to Samuel Ibn Nagrela, which is thought to have stood in the grounds of the Alhambra. What is generally accepted is that they were sculpted between the end of the X and beginning of the XI century.

Ceiling of the west pavillion

41

THE HALL OF THE ABENCERRAGES

It has been said that in Granada legend and history are so interwoven that it is impossible to distinguish between the two. The name "Abencerrage" is a mutation of *banu al-Sarrya*, the name of a family who played an important role in the politics of their day. Legend has it that a rival family, the "Zenete", engineered a conspiracy involving the sultana in an amorous affair and that in a fit of jealousy the sultan invited thirty-six men of the Abencerrage family to a celebration in this hall and had them all cut down in front of him. In fact it is not clear when this is supposed to have happened and the story has also been attributed to various sultans.

The story affirms that the russet veins in the marble in the bottom of the fountain are the bloodstains of the murdered courtiers. They are of course oxidisation in the marble itself.

This hall is an ideal refuge in the heat of summer. When

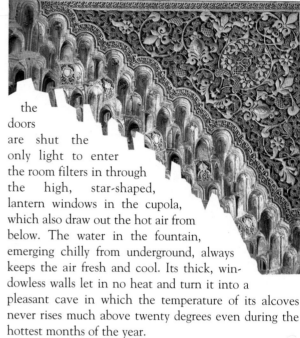

the doors are shut the only light to enter the room filters in through the high, star-shaped, lantern windows in the cupola, which also draw out the hot air from below. The water in the fountain, emerging chilly from underground, always keeps the air fresh and cool. Its thick, windowless walls let in no heat and turn it into a pleasant cave in which the temperature of its alcoves never rises much above twenty degrees even during the hottest months of the year.

The alcoves, set apart by pillars from the rest of the room, were reserved for couches and divans. The step up into these alcoves accentuates their separation from the rest of the room. They usually open onto a courtyard or another room but would have been curtained off for privacy.

THE HALL OF THE KINGS

This hall occupies the whole of the east side of the courtyard. It is divided into five separate areas; three of these are chambers illuminated from the porticos giving onto the courtyard and separated from each other by the other two transitional rooms, which lie in deep shadow. From either end the hall appears to be a succession of light and shade, each room is defined by high, pointed stucco arches, all elaborately decorated in different styles. This variety in adornment and the alternation of light and shade renders even such rich and complex decoration soothing

Left: from behind the fountain the perspective is one of a series of different brilliantly lit optical planes. Right in the background, through The Mirador of Lindaraja in the Hall of the Two Sisters there was a view of the old city framed against the sky. The surface of the fountain reflects the magnificent coffered ceiling, the muqarnas of which form an enormous eight-pointed star.

Fountain in the Hall of the Abencerrajes.

Ceiling in the Hall of the Abencerrajes

to the eye, without producing the fatigue which Baroque design can cause when repeated incessantly. The alcove of the central chamber, due to its privileged position, belonged without doubt to the sultan and his retinue. Sitting here the view of the courtyard appears to be one of an oasis seen through a grove of palm trees with the fountain of the lions at its centre.

The ceilings in the Hall of Kings reveal the great diversity of form which *muqarnas* can express. In fact the same element seems to alter throughout the day as the light thrown upon it changes in colour and angle. In this way the light becomes a primary component of the architecture itself.

The ceilings of the alcoves at the back of the three principal chambers are painted with pictures of seated kings and other human and animal forms. It is generally accepted that they date from the end of the XIV or beginning of the XV centuries. The paintings are on sheep skin stuck to wooden frames with starch glue and small bamboo pins to prevent their coming unstuck because of differences in expansion rates and also to avoid any damage that might be caused by rusty nails.

THE HALL OF THE TWO SISTERS

Contrary to what was believed until recently, it is now known that this hall is the oldest of all the rooms surrounding the Courtyard of the Lions. What this room was called originally is unknown but its present-day name, the Two Sisters, refers to the twin pair of Macael marble slabs that lie in the centre of the room.

Two sturdy arches on each side (east and west) of the main entrance from the courtyard provide access to sleeping alcoves. The arch in front leads out of the Hall

Domed ceiling in the Hall of the Two Sisters

of the Two Sisters proper into the Chamber of the Ajimeces (referring to the beautiful mullion windows), which itself serves as an anteroom to the Mirador of Lindaraja. Above these arches there are four more smaller ones which provide light for the rooms above. The pattern and metallic reflections of the tiles adorning the wainscot of this room are some of the most original and beautiful to be found in the whole of the Alhambra. The general pattern is one of small shields in a band surrounding a labyrinth of interwoven lines without beginning or end. As a counterpoint to this, the jambs to the arches (right) are decorated with circular motifs.

Above the walls the square design of the room is transformed into an octagon by the use of *muqarna* pendentives, upon which rests the ceiling, with two windows high up in each plane of the octagon. Until 1590 light was projected through these openings onto the *muqarnas* through stained-glass. The effect of the light upon the *muqarnas* was to give a sensation of movement, which the light imparted to the ceiling according to its angle of incidence at any moment. There are no two seconds in the day when the cupola looks exactly the same and its eternal mutation within unity represents a metaphor of the stars in the firmament circling around their northern axis.

Relationships between Muslims and Christians at this time were not always so tense as we are led to believe. At times they made alliances to help each other against third parties of either persuasion. A detail that reveals the importance of cultural exchange during the reign of Mohammad V is the repetitive design of the fleur de lys, the Bourbon symbol that Pedro I added to his arms when he married Blanche de Bourbon. It appears here either as a symbol of friendship or homage. This friendship incidentally caused the Castilian king, known as the Just, considerable problems during his reign.

"From the cosmological point of view the hemispherical cupola represented the sky with its constant spinning motion, whilst the cube of the walls and room below it represented the earthly world, ruled by contrast. The sky is ether. The cells comprising the *muqarnas* that form the transition from the seamless cupola to the square walls freeze the ether of the sky into the solidity of the earth. The stalactite effect is obtained by accentuating and elongating the groins of the vault, in which there may be several honeycombs of *muqarnas*. Furthermore, the honeycombs or individual cells of the design can be assembled in a multitude of ways, with convex and concave shapes. Granadan artists have dissolved entire vaults into *muqarna* honeycombs, the honey of which is the sky itself. A similar effect is produced by the fretworks and grilles carved into the front walls of the

MOSAICS: MYSTICISM AND MATHEMATICS

THE COMPOSITIONAL PRINCIPLES WHICH GUIDE THE ISLAMIC ORNAMENTAL CODE CAN BE REDUCED TO STYLISED, REPETITIVE RHYTHM. SUCH RHYTHM IS THE BASIC COMPOSITIONAL ELEMENT IN ALL ISLAMIC ART, INCLUDING POETRY AND MUSIC. IN THEIR ART ORNAMENTAL DESIGNS AND MOTIFS FOLLOW EACH OTHER IN REITERATIVE RHYTHMS TOWARDS INFINITY AS A METAPHOR OF ETERNITY, WHICH FILLS THE WHOLE OF SPACE. IT CONSISTS OF FORMULAS CREATED BY THE MULTIPLICATION, DIVISION, ROTATION AND SYMMETRICAL DISTRIBUTION OF BASIC, DECEPTIVELY SIMPLE THEMES.

A FASCINATION FOR REPETITION AND SYMMETRY AND THE CONTINUITY OF MOTIFS IS THE PRIME MOTIVATION IN ISLAMIC ART. THIS PRODUCES AN EFFECT WHICH IS DYNAMIC AND AT THE SAME TIME IMMUTABLE, IN WHICH EACH CONCEPT OF THE OVERALL DESIGN PRESERVES ITS OWN IDENTITY WITHOUT HOLDING SWAY OVER ANY OF THE OTHERS. NO DETAIL DOMINATES THE WHOLE: IT IS UNITY FORMED FROM MULTIPLICITY AND MULTIPLICITY IN ONE. THE RESULT IS COMPLETE HARMONY AND TRANQUILLITY, AN ART AT REST WHERE ALL TENSION IS DISSIPATED. (PROF. C. BORRÁS).

halls; the wall seems to be so transparent that it might be made of cells filled with light."
(*Titus Burckhardt*)

"... In the light all the materials shine and gleam; they glow luminously. As every individual note of colour in the decoration is quite small, the chromatic effect is one of pointillist fragmentation, weightless, absolutely incorporeal, the pure vibration of light in a diaphanous mantle, constantly changing its shape and colour .... the light as it shines on the surfaces from different angles creates contrasts in planes and textures and generates mobility in form. Artistic reality here, like reality in nature, appears at every moment to be newly shaped from myriads of atoms." (*Carlos Borrás*).

THE MIRADOR OF LINDARAJA

The name, "Lindaraja" would seem to derive from the phonetic mutation and semantic misunderstanding of three Arabic words, "ain-dar-Aixa" (the eyes of the house of Aixa). The mirador, in which the window sills are still at their original height, has a beautiful mullion window in its north wall, overlooking the garden of Lindaraja. Before the gallery that now encloses the garden was added on after the Christian conquest, the whole city could be seen beyond and below the wall. Crowning the mirador a stained-glass lantern window, fitted into a delicate wooden frame, filled this small room, once the throne room, with multi-coloured light. All the dados in this room are made out of tiny hand-made tiles. In the embellishment covering the jambs of the arch are splendid inscriptions in black ceramic fixed upon a white background. They allude to Muhammad V and are without doubt the finest and most laboriously executed in the palace, a masterpiece of Muslim art.

Arches forming the entrance to the Hall of the Two Sisters

Los Baños

The Bath-house

The bath-house of the Comares Palace had a very specific function directly related to politics and diplomacy. The position of its door, the first on the left in the eastern wall of the Courtyard of the Myrtles, close to the entrance to the Hall of the Ambassadors, betrays its use: it was a comfortable place to conduct the friendly management of official business. Thus it was not in constant use but only when it was thought necessary to gain the friendship and favour of visiting dignitaries and diplomats from other kingdoms.

The Arabs took the layout of their baths from the Roman thermae. From them they inherited the characteristic division into a cool room (frigidarium)), warm room (tepidarium)) and hot room (calidarium), and adapted the concept to their own taste and architectural styles.

Apart from his obligatory ritual ablutions, bathing has a very important place in the life of a Muslim; he usually washes both before and after meals, whenever he touches a dirty object, after using the lavatory and of course before touching the Koran. Throughout the history of Islam, the public bath has been second only to the mosque as a focal point of social life and had the same influence on mediaeval urban activity as the agora in ancient Greece or the town square in Western society.

JARDINES DEL PARTAL

TORRE DE LAS DAMAS

PARTAL

El Partal

El Generalife

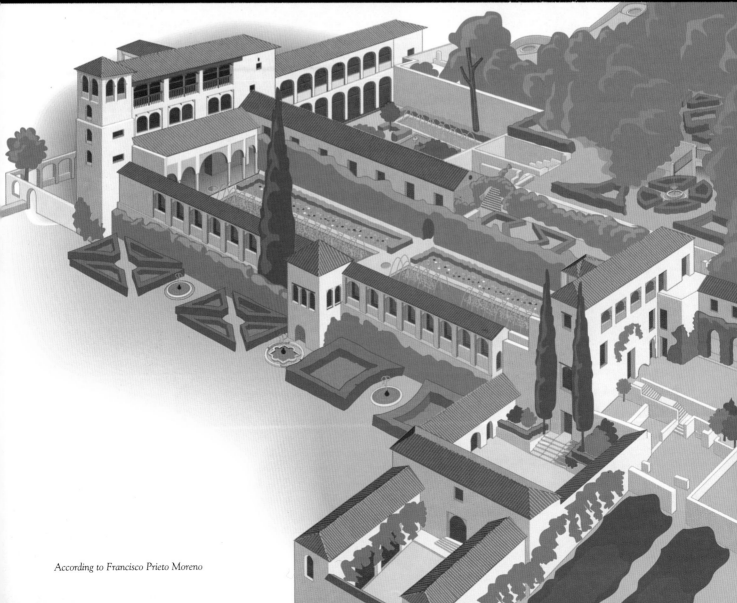

According to Francisco Prieto Moreno

THE GENERALIFE

Of the many private houses with gardens and orchards that once graced the slopes of the Hill of the Sun this is the only one remaining.

The Generalife was a retreat where the sultan could relax, away from the daily toil and bustle of the court. Nevertheless, its proximity to the Alhambra meant that he could still be close enough to palace affairs to attend to any urgent matter which might arise, whilst at the same time be far enough away to enjoy the intimacy of the countryside.

The land around the Generalife was always cultivated; it took pride of place among many such outlying farmsteads owned by the sultan. Fortunately its orchard terraces have survived relatively unchanged to this day.

Outside the buildings all that remains of the original gardens are the cultivated, orchard terraces. These terraced gardens climbed to the very top of the hill, and looking from above a single garden seemed to stretch endlessly all the way down, a garden of an infinite variety of colours, carefully planned by the skilful planting of mixtures of ornamental and fruit trees on every terrace.

The planting of the present-day gardens was begun in 1931 and finished in 1951 under the care of Francisco Prieto Moreno, and although they may not closely resemble those of the middle ages they undoubtedly lend beauty and dignity to an area that was in a seriously neglected state. In replanting the gardens, cypresses, myrtles and box were used for the hedges; rambling roses, vines and oleander to climb pillars and cover pergolas in the upper walk, and elsewhere, an abundance of other species of trees - oranges, plums, medlars and magnolias were planted amidst a profusion of bushes and flowers, so that the gardens contain in all some 160 different species.

The walks are paved in traditional Granadan style: a mosaic of small pebbles, white ones from the river Darro and black from the river Genil. Paving of this sort is still laid in courtyards and squares throughout the city.

In the words of Professor Manzano, the Generalife was at one and the same time a *djennat*, or paradise, and an orchard or garden which supplied the Royal House with provisions. "An orchard is only a frag-

The Water-Garden in summer

The Water-Garden in Autumn

ment of nature, carefully walled off from a dry or even desert exterior, which is always hostile to man. The space inside the walls, irrigated and brought to life with water, has been geometrically laid out and planted with trees and carefully selected bushes and flowers to make it into a domestic environment, leafy, fragrantly perfumed, a true image of *djennat*, or paradise on earth". It does not attain the dimensions of the great oriental *hairs* of the Umayyad princes, with their hunting reserves, which certainly also existed in Granada, attached to palaces built farther outside the city beyond the hill upon which the Generalife is built. This type of royal garden existed as a contrast to the urban palace in all the courts of emirs, caliphs and minor *taifa* kings throughout the history of Islamic Spain.

The Muslim garden was to be enjoyed with all the senses: the sight and smell of the flowers, the sound of water and the feel and taste of fruit as they were picked from the trees while walking beneath them.

THE WATER-GARDEN COURTYARD

Despite being the oldest of the palaces and having undergone substantial alterations, this is possibly the area of the Alhambra which best preserves the style of the mediaeval garden in al-Andalus. In its original conception it relied upon the normal plan of an elongated courtyard with a pool to reflect the surrounding façades. The later addition of water spouts has broken up the surface of the mirror. The west wall would have had no openings save the small mirador, following the tradition of "a closed paradise", invisible from outside and turned in upon itself, a tradition which dominated Andalusian architectural design.

The original concept was that water trickling into the pool from the two fountains at either end would make a gentle murmur, like soothing music, the most pleasant of sounds apart from silence to encourage meditative thought. The rationalists of the eighteenth century age of reason, however, and above all

El Jardín

The Spanish-Muslim Garden

To situate a house within a garden you should select a rise in the ground to make it easier to guard. The building should be at the entrance to the property and orientated towards midday, and the well or irrigation tank should be sited at the highest point of all. Better still than a well is to dig a channel which should run in the shade of the plants and trees. Plant clumps of all sorts of evergreens close to the channel to delight the eye, and, a little farther away, as wide a variety of flowers and evergreen trees as possible. A vineyard should surround the garden whilst in the middle climbing vines provide shade for the paths between the flower beds. At the very centre you should erect an open pavilion for the hours of rest, surrounded by climbing roses, myrtles and other varieties of flower to beautify the view. The garden should be longer than it is wide so as not to tire the eyes in contemplation. A room should be built at the lower end for guests. Make a pool hidden between the trees so that it might not be seen from a distance. It is also useful to build a dovecote and a habitable tower. The house itself should have two doors so as to be more easily protected and the owner feel secure.

Ibn Luyun, Treatise on Agriculture and Gardening

Overall view of the Water-Garden

the romantics of the following century, imposed their own vision and taste, replacing the sonorous silence and gentle, natural flow of water with artificial splashing.

After a fire in 1958 the original design of this courtyard was discovered and recon-structed. It is the focal point of the whole residence and a perfect example of a Spanish-Muslim gar-den. During this restoration some jets were put in, which, at the last resort, might be said to imitate the music of rain falling.

The arches provide access into a transverse chamber with a carved, wooden ribbon-work ceiling. The position of this room at the far end of the courtyard and the presence of niches for ritual jugs of water (left) suggest that this was the sultan's reception room.

The chamber finishes in a mirador added during the reign of Ismail I (1319), slightly angled to the right compared to the central axis of the pool, as can be seen in the photograph. In fact the whole pavilion is a few degrees out of line with the courtyard. It is quite diffi-cult to comprehend how in the hottest months the north mirador always catches a breeze to relieve the suffocating heat of midday. Doubtless there is a combination of factors to explain this phe-nomenon, the secrets of which the master builder was well aware: the situation, the height, the orienta-tion, so perfect throughout the Alhambra, and here in this mirador, just slightly slanted off centre to achieve that breath of air which surpris-es us so much today. It provides an object lesson for architects of the twenty-first centu-ry, who are striving to integrate nature into their buildings and create microclimates, even within closed spaces, to relieve the weight of concrete and the visual aggression of cement. A poem written on a lapislazuli background (below) runs above the arches. It is dedicated to the sultan Abu I-Walid Ismail and the reference to the year of "the great

triumph for religion" places the decorative work in the year 1319.

THE COURTYARD OF THE CYPRESS

The original layout and appearance of this courtyard is not completely clear. The U-shaped pool is not Nasrid, as in 1526 the Venetian ambassador, Andrea Navaggiero, described this court as being, "like a meadow with trees", which was irrigated regularly by some ingenious system that brought the water as though from nowhere. It is also known as the Courtyard of the Sultana, because of the legend of the sultana who arranged her trysts here with one of the Abencerrages, an affair which led to the massacre of all the men of that family.

THE UPPER GARDENS.

This delightful example of a romantic garden was laid out here after the French invasion, over the abandoned remains of the original gardens. A magnificent wisteria overhangs the path down from the romantic mirador (left). Below, a fountain set among box hedges in one of the middle terraces.

THE WATER STAIRWAY

This is one of the few genuine Nasrid features to be preserved in this part of the gardens. The Muslim obsession with water led them to the extreme of creating a liquid hand rail. If there had in fact been a small oratory at the top of the steps, as has been suggested, this could have served for the ritual hand-washing.

THE CYPRESS WALK

Cypress trees have always been associated with cemeteries, particularly since the Romantic period, for the good reason that their roots grow straight and deep and don't break into the tombs. Muslim architects favoured the cypress for the same reason: it seeks water at depth and can be planted closely to form a dense evergreen screen.

OPEN-AIR CONCERT ARENA

In 1952 this amphitheatre was built upon the ruins of old agricultural outbuildings. The sunken arena provides an ideal setting for ballet and dance, particularly during the annual Festival of Music and Dance, and many famous ballerinas, such as Margot Fonteyn among others, have performed here.

Seville orange
Citrus auranteum ver. Amara

Scented waterlily
Nymphaea ordorata

Golden-rain tree
Koelreuteria
paniculata

Wistaria
Wisteria sinensis

Blanket flower
Gaillardia pulchella

African lily, *Agapanthus africanus*

Hybrid rose, *Rosa hybr.*

Cockscomb, *Celosia cristata*

Statice, Everlasting flowers, *Statice fruticans &*
Blanket flower, *Gaillaria aristata*

Hibiscus
Hibiscus rosa sinensis

Oleander, *Nerium oleander*

Delphinium
Delphinium hybr.

Snowball, *Viburnum opulus*

Scarlet sage, *Salvia splendens*

Pansy, *Viola wittrockiana*

El Palacio de Carlos V

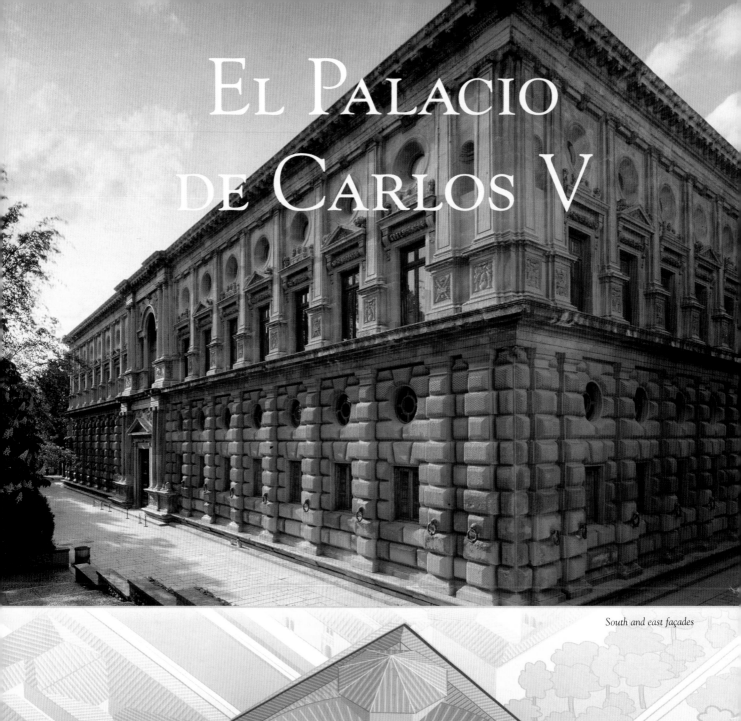

South and east façades

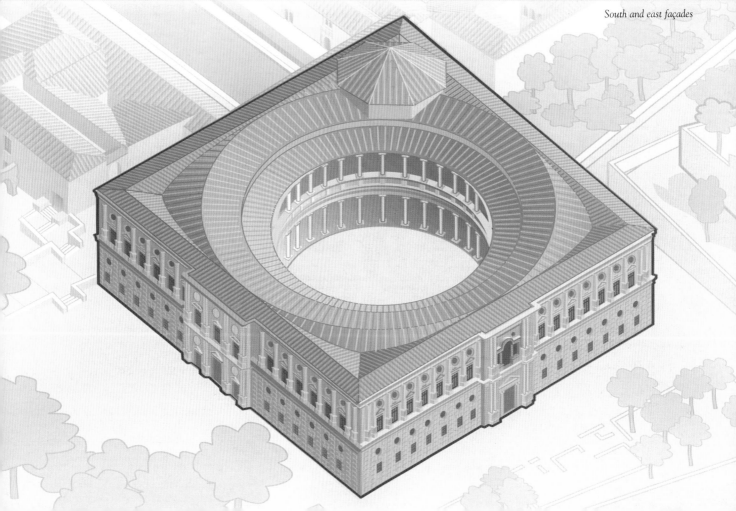

The Palace of Charles V

If there exists any one monument so controversial and misunderstood, and yet so often referred to as outstanding, it is the Palace of Charles V. Romantic clichés vilified it as an attempt by authoritarian Spanish monarchs to erase the Muslim past but a more dispassionate look at history will reveal the great symbolic value with which the Spanish monarchy invested the conquest of Granada, and their political determination to reinforce Granada's role as a capital city, which it had enjoyed for so many centuries, by building great new monuments without destroying the old, complementing rather than detracting from the past. The new palace was in fact built upon an old Christian quarter, a lower annex to the Nasrid city, rather than at the expense of knocking down the existing Muslim palaces, although an error in geometry meant that its design would encroach very slightly upon the Comares tower. Within this context, however, it might be worth trying to understand the reasons behind such a new and radical project.

In 1526 the young King Charles I of Spain, the Holy Roman Emperor Charles V, married his cousin Isabel of Portugal in Sevilla, at that time one of the most important mercantile cities in Europe. But in recognition of his grandparents' affection for Granada, he included the city in his ceremonial honeymoon procession. During their official visit to Granada the royal couple stayed in a suite of rooms surrounding the mirador of Lindaraja in the Alhambra, which still bears the name, "the lodgings of Charles V" (and incidentally were the rooms chosen by later visitors to the Alhambra, such as Washington Irving and Richard Ford). It was here that the future King Phillip II was conceived, although Queen Isabel, frightened by an earthquake in August 1526, decided she would be safer in the newly built Jeronimite monastery in the city below.

The Catholic monarchs had already built their funerary chapel in Granada, the Royal Chapel, and the young emperor during his stay in Granada showed his keenness to ennoble the city still further. He took personal interest in many building projects, such as the new cathedral in the city centre and the royal hospital just outside the Elvira gate.

The emperor entrusted the building of his new palace alongside the Muslim royal houses in the Alhambra to the Marquis of Mondéjar, governor of the Alhambra, but he left no specific orders as to the design or to the way the work should be carried out. The Marquis of Mondéjar was a scion of the noble family of Mendoza, of Toledo, who had contributed towards spreading an appreciation of Italian Renaissance art throughout Spain. Not surprisingly therefore, the architecture of the new palace epitomises these innovative Renaissance concepts of ingenuity and variety of form. But Andalucía, thanks to the double influence of Sevilla (the centre of commerce with the West Indies) and Granada (the symbolic capital of the centuries-long battle against the world of Islam), was also particularly receptive to the influx of these new Renaissance trends, a style called at the time "Roman". Nevertheless, the palace will always be the symbol of a reign that began with so much zest for achievement and grand projects which in the end would never be entirely accomplished. (It should be remembered, for example, that the roof over the second floor of this palace was only put on in the XX century.)

Charles' presence in Granada and his ambitious building plans led to the city's becoming a focus of attraction for architects and artists from far and wide, not just from Spain but from Italy and Holland. It attracted Diego de Siloë, for example, who arrived here in about 1528 and whose hand can be seen in almost every building thereafter, particularly the cathedral and the royal hospital. But the design and construction of the new royal palace was entrusted to a fairly unknown young architect named Pedro Machuca, who had arrived some years earlier with Jacobo Florentino from Italy. Machuca had spent his youth in Florence and ostensibly had had a solid apprentice-

The central, circular courtyard

The western façade

ship in Rome, working with both Michael Angelo and Rafael. Thanks to this training he would have known in theory about the most elaborate creations of such Renaissance architects as Bramante. Proof of this lies in his choice of the very singular design of a round courtyard within a square building, which had been the basis of the highest aspirations of ideal design since the days of Alberti. In fact Machuca's credentials are somewhat hazy: there is no record of his ever having reached the grade of Master Architect and the work he was engaged upon before being entrusted with the palace was of a fairly routine sort in the Alhambra. But he could count on the patronage of Luis Hurtado de Mendoza, Count of Tendilla and governor of the Alhambra, whom he had served as squire in 1526 and with whom he seems to have struck up a certain degree of personal friendship (It is believed that his son Luis was named after his patron.). Whatever his origins, he had learnt well in Italy and his natural flair for design led him to build a palace that would immortalise him as an architect. When Pedro Machuca died in 1550 he was succeeded by his son Luis and later by Juan de Orea, who worked under the supervision of

Juan de Herrera as far as the design of the stairs and the upper part of the main doorway were concerned. This building phase finished under the direction of Minjares.

Machuca was originally commissioned to carry out the work with funds that Charles' grandparents, the Catholic Monarchs, had bequeathed towards the repair of the old Moorish palaces, together with 80,000 ducats, which the emperor had received in taxes from the *Moriscos* of his kingdom. This latter source of finance posed two problems: firstly, the *Moriscos* had to surrender sums of money which before this, according to the most informed functionaries of the time, had been devoted to hospitals and public welfare, thus resulting in the incongruent situation that the Christian king was using public welfare money to build his own house; and secondly, the *Morisco* uprising in 1568, one of the cruellest of civil wars, ruined the kingdom of Granada for ever after, and this was to impede the original project's ever coming to fruition. After the 1550's the emperor's interest in his palace in the Alhambra began to decline. Also his son, Philip II, who was

70

Stairway in the south-eastern curvature

crowned king in 1556, was more interested in building his own palace, the Escorial, near Madrid, relegating the palace in the Alhambra to a project of secondary importance. Successive delays, almost always due to a lack of funds, resulted in the palace's remaining unfinished up to the present day.

Machuca must have found inspiration for his overall plan of the palace, a circular courtyard within a square building, from the Tempietto next to San Pietro in Montorio in Rome, which includes a circular colonnade around an inner square chapel, all of which was to have been surrounded by a circular courtyard. Similar round courtyards are to be seen in the Villa Madama by Rafael and in drawings by Leonardo da Vinci.

The solution of the rounded architrave is completely original in this palace, creating as it does a perfect relationship between force and resistance in the two compositional elements. The annulet is supported in a torus (the curved vault of the gallery) which resists the outward thrust of the stone as though it were a a continuous flying buttress, one foot of which is supported in the annulet and the other in the wall. When the wall is weakened by the presence of a door, as is in the west wall, the strength of the outer wall is augmented by a depressed vault or with buttresses of some other kind.

From the outside there are clear differences in the style of the lower and upper floors. The lower floor has the robustness of a medieval castle with the characteristic rustication of the stone pillars so beloved of the Florentines, whilst the first floor shows a tendency towards the Mannerism of Juan Herrera; for example, the illusion of walls of greater thickness produced by the circular, conical clerestory lights over the windows. The most notable features on the main western façade are the two winged female forms reclining on the tympanum, carved in marble by the Flemish artist Antonio de Leval. The same sculptor was responsible for the cherubs above the tympana of the side doors, the medallions with Flemish warriors on them and the unfinished grey stone lions flanking the doorway in the south façade. The right-hand relief, representing the battle of Pavia (in which everyone is left-handed) has also been attributed by some scholars to Leval but it is more likely to be the work of Pedro Machuca. The left-hand relief (where everyone is right-handed) is by Juan de Orea. All the other reliefs are allusions to the Triumph of Peace, with angels burning flags and the tools of war in a desire for disarmament. The upper tier of the façade is neither so richly decorated nor so interesting. It gives the impression that the original design was simplified to the minimum. Two medallions by Ocampo of the trials of Hercules are worthy of note. In fact, all the sculptures present a clear imperial message to the conquered city concerning the figure of the emperor, often sculpted as Caesar. The original project envisaged the west and south façades preceded by squares surrounded by pillared galleries but these were left unmade. The palace was never finished and never occupied by Charles. Today it houses the Alhambra museum and is used during the Festival of Music and dance to stage concerts.

Reliefs adorning the western façade

The two bodies of the south façade are in splendid harmony, although the reliefs by Nicolao di Corte are not so inspired as those on the main façade.

The interior of the palace is arranged into large halls around the side, except in the north-west curvature, where the chapel and the crypt are housed. The chapel was in fact the most important aspect of the palace as far as Charles was concerned. On 30 November 1527, on receiving the projected design, he wrote, "I only want to ask that the hall at the front be large and that there be a chapel in it to say and hear mass." But in this original plan the new Royal House could already be seen as a theatrical aggrandisement of the older dwellings of the Nasrid city. The interior, with its courtyard forty-two metres in diameter and containing thirty-two monumental pillars of mauve porphyry (pudding stone), is characterised by its completely sober austerity: two floors with Doric and Tuscan lintels and a great stairway which joins the magnificent annular barrel vault over the vestibule.

The upper level of the court, with ionic columns of the same stone as those on the ground floor, was roofed in 1967 with a wooden coffered ceiling. The beams and deep box-moulding could easily have been the work of Pedro Machuca himself. The same is true of the staircase in the southeast corner leading to the fine-arts museum, which with its bold curves far surpasses the seventeenth century one in the opposite corner, despite its modernity. Attempts have been made to find precedents for the plan of this building and it has been suggested that it might have been inspired by the Palace of Caprarola by Vignola, but in fact Machuca's palace predates Vignola's by almost twenty years.

The crypt is to be found under the unfinished chapel in the north-east curve of the courtyard. It is now reached by a stairway in the vestibule on the east side. It has a star-shaped octagonal vault, almost flat in section, with no other form of support other than its own curvature and can rightly be considered one of the works of genius of the Renaissance.

As a parting thought, any visitor to the Alhambra should bear in mind that it is probably thanks to the existence of the Palace of Charles V that the Alhambra itself came to be included in the patrimony of Spanish Royal Palaces instead of being reduced to an archaeological remnant of a defeated culture.

Reliefs adorning the main doorway in the southern façade

The main hall of the mercantile exchange, a Gothic structure adjoining the Royal Chapel (S. XVI), with a painting of the Surrender of Pradilla in the centre, flanked by portraits of the Catholic King and Queen.

GRANADA IN CHRISTIAN TIMES

At the end of the XV century the Iberian Peninsula, like the rest of Europe, was a patchwork of states constantly feuding with each other to achieve regional dominion. Castilla, whose domains spread from the Sea of Cantabria in the north to Gibraltar in the south, was at this time the ruling power in Spain; Aragón occupied the north-west corner of the peninsula and turned its attention towards the Mediterranean, whilst the Muslim kingdom of Granada, ruled by the Nasrid dynasty, was ensconced in the mountains to the south-east. Portugal, which had been an independent country for more than a century, held sway over the Atlantic seaboard, leaving Navarra in the Pyrenees to play off its more powerful surrounding neighbours, France, Aragón and Castilla, against each other. Throughout the XV century Castilla and Aragón had been through periods of war and truce, in all of which the aristocratic families of both states played an important role, taking advantage of the relative weakness of their monarchs. But the marriage of Ferdinand of Aragón to Isabel of Castilla in 1469 united the two kingdoms and gave the young monarchs sufficient power to bring the rebel aristocrats to heel and channel their bellicose energy into the war against the kingdom of Granada. Thus, within a relatively short time the structure of the whole country took a new shape and entered into the modern age.

After pacifying their own kingdoms and assuring the neutrality of Portugal, which had aspirations to the crown of Castilla itself, Ferdinand and Isabel concentrated their efforts on their long-held ambition to conquer the Moorish kingdom of Granada, which they undertook with all the fervour of a crusade, thus bringing them the invaluable aid of foreign troops as well as uniting their own kingdoms

behind them. The war against Granada, the final frontier war between Christians and Muslims, went on for ten years, from 1481 to 1492, and was at one and the same time the last chivalric war in Spain and the first modern one, in which periodic fair-weather skirmishes gave way to well defined strategic planning based on the efficient marshalling of troops, new armaments and overall military and numerical supremacy. The conquest of Granada was hailed as a great triumph throughout Christendom and compensated to some extent the fall of Constantinople to the Turks fifty years before. It restored morale to a Christian world overshadowed by the emerging power of the Ottoman empire, which was shortly to threaten Europe itself by laying siege to Vienna.

The occupation of Granada by the Catholic Monarchs, Ferdinand and Isabel, on 2 January 1492 marked the beginning of the modern age and a complete change of direction in the futures of both Spain and Europe. Granada was the last Muslim kingdom to be conquered and its symbolic past led the Catholic Monarchs to turn it into the centre of their new Christian state, a state which would soon make its influence felt in European politics and set in motion the great adventure of the Americas. This in turn was to draw attention away from the familiar area of the Mediterranean and direct it towards the Atlantic, and although the Turkish and Italian problems would still continue to trouble the minds of Spanish kings for some time to come they were now in a position to play an important role in the formation of the new Europe.

Many of these events, so crucial to the future of Spain and Europe, occurred in and around the places described in this book

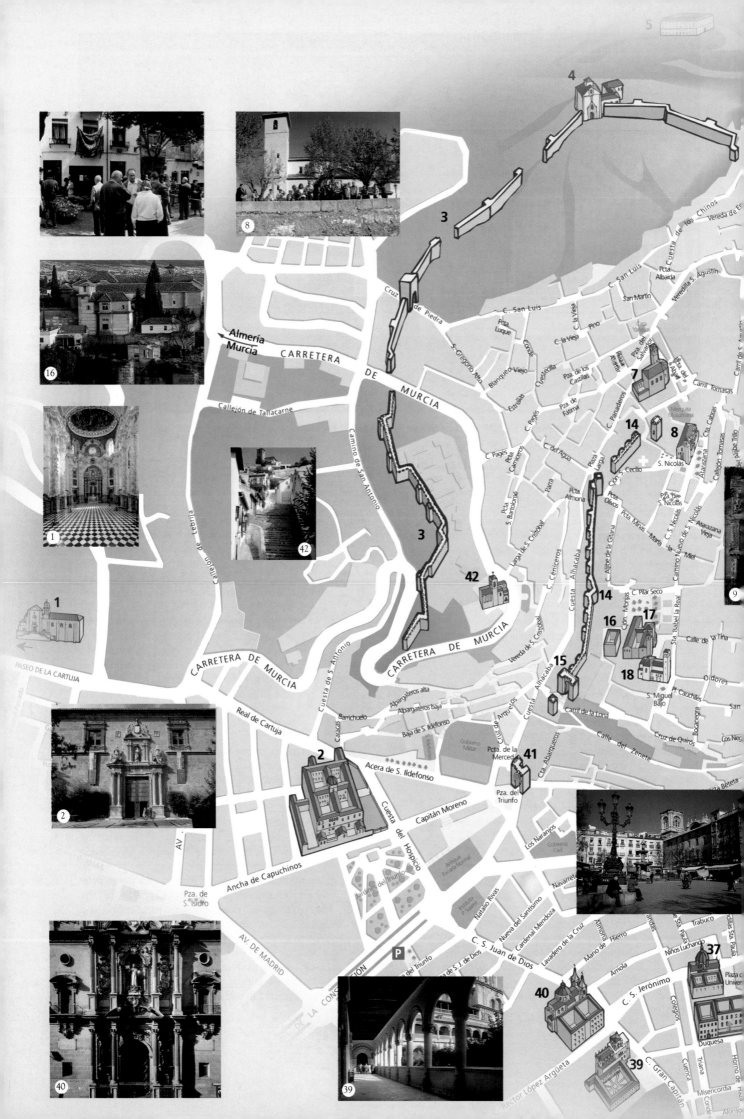

4

3

8

16

1

42

1

3

42

14

Almería
Murcia

CARRETERA

DE MURCIA

Callejón de Tallacarne

Camino de San Antonio

Callejón de Lebrija

PASEO DE LA CARTUJA

CARRETERA DE MURCIA

CARRETERA DE MURCIA

C. San Luis

Pcta. del Albaida
Veredilla S. Agustín

San Martín

C. San Luis

Pcta. Luque

Conde

C. la Vieja

Pino

Carril Tomasas

Estrellas

C. Pagés

Cuestecilla

Blanqueo Viejo

Pza. de los Castillas

Plaza del Salvador

Mezquita Musulmana

7

C. Pagés

Pcta. Carniceros

Pza. de Fátima

C. del Agua

C. Panaderos

14

8

S. Nicolás

Pcta. S. Bartolomé

Parra

Pza. Larga

Cmn. S. Cecilio

Atarazana

Callejón Tomasas

Pcta. Almona

Pcta. Olivos

Pza. de S. Nicolás

C. S. Nicolás

Atarazana Vieja

Cuesta Alhacaba

C. Aljibe de la Gitana

C. Cerniceros

Marfa la

Miel

9

14

C. Pilar Seco

Cjon. Monjas

17

Sta. Isabel la Real

Calle de la Tiña

16

Vereda de S. Cristóbal

15

Carril de la Lona

18

Oidores

S. Miguel Bajo

Pl. Cauchiles

San

Cuesta Alhacaba

Cruz de Quirós

Calle del Zenete

Real de Cartuja

Alpargateros alta

Alpargateros baja

Baja de S. Ildefonso

Barrichuelo

Calados

Cuesta de S. Antonio

Gobierno Militar

Cruz de Arqueros

Pcta. de la Merced

41

Pza. del Triunfo

2

Acera de S. Ildefonso

Cuesta del Hospicio

Capitán Moreno

2

AV.

Pza. de S. Isidro

Ancha de Capuchinos

Antigua Escuela Normal

Jardines del Triunfo

Instituto P. Suárez

Los Naranjos

Gobierno Civil

Navarrete

AV. DE MADRID

P

del Triunfo

C. S. J. de Dios

Natalio Rivas

Nueva del Santísimo

Cardenal Mendoza

C. S. Juan de Dios

Lavadero de la Cruz

Almona de Hierro

Mano de

Arriola

Sta. Paula

Trabuco

Niños Luchando

37

Plaza de Univers

DE LA CONSTITUCIÓN

Rector López Argüeta

40

C. S. Jerónimo

Colegios

39

C. Gran Capitán

Duquesa

Triana

Horno de

Cuerva

Misericordia

40

39

1. Monasterio de la Cartuja (S. XVI-XVIII)
2. Hospital Real (s. XVI-XVII)
3. Muralla Nazarí (s. XIV-XV)
4. Ermita de S. Miguel Alto
5. Abadía del Sacromonte (s. XVII)
6. Palacio de los Córdova
7. Iglesia del Salvador (antigua Mezquita)
8. Iglesia de S. Nicolás (s. XVI)
9. Casa de Castril. Museo Arqueológico
10. Iglesia de S. Pedro (s. XVI)
11. Convento Sta. Catalina (s. XVI)
12. Baño árabe del Bañuelo (s. XI)
13. Puente del Cadí (s. XIII)
14. Muralla Zirí (s. XI)
15. Puerta de Monaita (s. XI)
16. Palacio de Dar-al-Horra (s. XV)
17. Convento de Sta. Isabel la Real (s. XVI)
18. Iglesia de S. Miguel Bajo (s. XVI)
19. Minarete de S. José (s. X)
20. Iglesia de Sta. Ana (s. XVI)
21. Real Chancillería (s. XVI)
22. Puerta de las Granadas (s. XVI)
23. Torres Bermejas (s. XII-XV)
24. Casa de los Tiros (s. XVI)
25. Casa árabe de los Girones (s.XIII)
26. Iglesia de S. Matías (s. XVI)
27. Iglesia de Sto. Domingo (s. XVII)
28. Iglesia Comendadoras de Santiago
29. Iglesia de S. Cecilio (s. XVI)
30. Carmen de los Mártires (s. XIX)
31. Basílica. de las Angustias (s. XVII)
32. Corral del Carbón (alhóndiga s. XIV)
33. Alcaicería (s. XIV-XIX)
34. Madrasa (escuela coránica) (s. XIV-XVI)
35. Palacio de la Curia
36. Catedral, Capilla Real, Iglesia del Sagrario (s. XVI-XVIII)
37. Iglesia de S. Justo y Pastor (s. XVII)
38. Universidad Vieja (s. XVII), Jardín Botánico
39. Monasterio de S. Jerónimo (s. XVI)
40. Igl. y Hospital S. Juan de Dios (s. XVI-XVIII)
41. Puerta de Elvira (s. XI)

75

CAPILLA REAL

THE ROYAL CHAPEL:

THE NEW ERA All the sovereigns and grandees of this period made elaborate preparations during their lives for their own interment and so the architecture of this century is filled with magnificent funerary chapels. The Catholic Monarchs had founded the Church of San Juan de los Reyes (St. John of the Kings) in Toledo for just such a purpose but after the conquest of Granada they decided to build a chapel in the heart of their new domains, just beside the main mosque of the defeated Muslims and the site of the new Christian cathedral. On making this decision they clearly imposed a new spirit and new direction upon the city. The Royal Chapel was intended as a monument to celebrate their success and give thanks to God for bestowing upon them such a triumphant victory. In a royal warrant of 1504 Queen Isabel expressed her desire that her final resting place should be in Granada and set out in her will that this chapel be built at the expense of her estate. This was the first of many such plans which were to ennoble the city with impressive monumental buildings. New architectural fashions and perspectives were overtaking late-Gothic traditions and Granada offered an ideal *tabula rasa* upon which to execute these new schemes.

Not long after the conquest, during the early years of the XVI century, more than a hundred master craftsmen arrived in Spain from the Low Countries, easily recognisable by their names (Siloë, Egas and Vigamy, among others), and also from Italy, where they had been working on both civil and religious projects. Artistic tensions were aroused by modern building projects such as the Royal Chapel and the Cathedral, emblems of a new socio-political reality and symbols of the conquering powers. Two clear artistic tendencies existed side by side: the conservative Gothic, favoured by Queen Isabel and her clergy, lead by Cardinal Cisneros, a man opposed to the pagan novelties of Italian fashion, and the progressive Classic, which was more to the taste of King Ferdinand and the enlightened nobility, who were fond of the neo-Platonic, Romanesque style, which presumed to make a bridge between classical culture and the Catholic church. Some prelates who were familiar with Italian culture also supported Renaissance trends and used their influence on Charles V, whose wishes made Granada the foremost centre of art and architecture of the time, bringing together in the city the most outstanding artists of the day.

Statues of the Catholic Monarchs at prayer, attributed to Felipe de Vigarrey, the sculptor of the main altar piece of the Royal Chapel, for which they were originally made, although replaced afterwards by others sculpted by Diego de Siloë, which remain to this day. The abundance of extant portraits of the Catholic King and Queen and the closeness in time of the sculptures make it quite probable that these are fair likenesses, although possibly somewhat idealised. Their attitude in prayer gives them an air of serene majesty, which is emphasised by their ceremonial robes, all firmly within the tenets of the Renaissance style of exalting their fame and glorifying their triumphs.

THE CHURCH HAS ONE SINGLE NAVE DOMINATED BY AN IMPOSING GRILLE, WHICH FORMS A CLEAR DIVISION WITHIN THE HOLY PRECINCT, AS IS TYPICAL OF MANY SUCH ROYAL AND ARISTOCRATIC FUNEREAL CHAPELS OF THE XV CENTURY. IT WAS WROUGHT IN 1520 BY THE MOST FAMOUS MASTER CRAFTSMAN OF THE CENTURY, MASTER BARTOLOMÉ DE JAÉN, WHO SPENT TWO YEARS IN FORGING IT, DURING WHICH TIME THE EVOLUTION OF CONTEMPORARY IDEAS AND THE FUSING OF STYLES ARE VERY EVIDENT IN ITS FORM. SUCH SYNTHESES OF STYLE ARE COMMON THROUGHOUT THE ROYAL CHAPEL. FLOWERING FORTH FROM A TYPICALLY MEDIEVAL FRAMEWORK OF TWISTED IRON BARS ARE EMBOSSED AND GILDED RENAISSANCE ADORNMENTS THAT RESEMBLE THE WORK OF SILVERSMITHS AND MAKE THIS GRILLE A MODEL FOR THE STYLE WHICH BECAME KNOWN FOR THIS REASON AS "PLATERESQUE". IN THE SURMOUNTING CRESTING IS A SPLENDID REPRESENTATION OF THE PASSION, CONTAINING PERSONALITIES OF THE TIME, IN WHICH THE EXECUTIONERS ARE PICTURED AS BEING JEWS (RECENTLY EXPELLED FROM THE KINGDOM) RATHER THAN ROMANS.

It was constructed between 1505 and 1521, not without frequent indecision and changes of plan, by master builders Juan Gil de Hontañón and Juan de Álava, although eventually neither the originally planned cloister nor the main façade were built and the Royal Chapel was wedged in between the mercantile exchange, which now serves as its entrance, and the church of the Holy Shrine, which stands upon the site of the erstwhile Muslim mosque. All that can be seen of the Royal Chapel's exterior nowadays is the Renaissance doorway, designed by Juan García de Praves upon the personal orders of Charles V in 1526 (left), which contrasts markedly with the nearby Gothic windows and splendid flamboyant Gothic cresting (below). Inside, the harmonious disposition of volume, the tracery of the vaulting and the inscriptions referring to the king and queen, together with the polychromed shields, which fulfil symbolic as well as ornamental roles, have led scholars such as Professor Pita Andrade to claim that this chapel is one of the last and finest fruits of Gothic architecture in Spain (right).

For almost thirty years the Catholic Monarchs had constructed churches and monasteries in their own distinctive style, known as "Isabeline", which fused elements of late-Gothic tradition with Plateresque ornamentation. The Royal Chapel, designed by the master builder Enrique Egas, was true to this tradition of a church with a single nave, side chapels and a raised choir, culminating in a raised trapezoid main chapel. The queen herself had expressed her desire that her final resting place should be of "Franciscan simplicity", which restricted the architects in their original design and ultimately failed to satisfy their grandson Charles V, who called it "cramped" and "unsuitable for royalty". Destined to form part of a greater whole joined to the cathedral, its place as both chapel and pantheon led to later additions being made to its ornamentation: ironwork grilles, a main altar and catafalques, all of which raised its status and made it more suitable for the exaltation of the new monarchy.

On the left, a view of the mausoleum from above. Below, the arms of the Catholic Monarchs, *bearing the eagle of St. John the Evangelist and their own symbols, the yoke and arrows.*

Above and opposite, the catafalques of the Catholic Monarchs by Domenico Alessandro Fancelli.

King Ferdinand, whilst being against any over-elaboration in the design of the chapel, did not hesitate to take the Count of Tendilla's advice and choose the Florentine Domenico Alessandro Fancelli to design his cenotaph. Fancelli made it his masterpiece.

According to Pita Andrade, "Here we find the epitome of

In ancient times the griffin (left) symbolised strength and watchfulness, whilst for Christians it was a negative force representing only cruelty. Nevertheless, here, according to Professor Sánchez Mesa, the griffin might be interpreted as representing the triumph of Christianity over paganism. Above is a silver-gilt crown belonging to Queen Isabel and to the right her vellum missal.

XV century Florentine Renaissance, free-standing funerary sculpture ... it imbues the architecture of the Royal Chapel with a harmonious balance between the purely ornamental (griffins, wreaths and grotesques) and those religious elements which emphasise the transcendental nature of life on earth.".The Fathers of the Church, who surround the sepulchre, and the religious motifs (baptism, resurrection etc.) act as a counterpoint to the decorative and heraldic devices (St. George and Santiago), the former symbolising the triumph of the soul over death and the latter its triumph over the body. The catafalque is a truncated pyramid sculpted from Carrara marble, its wide base representing the extent of earthly domains and the fine, narrow border around its upper rim symbolising the limits of all human aspirations.

The figure of the queen is clothed in a simple tunic and mantle and she wears the Cross of Santiago around her neck. The king is in full armour and clasps a sword to his breast. According to Gómez Moreno, "The natural physiognomy of the king could only have been sculpted from life, whereas that of the queen is much less lifelike."

To the left is a gilded, embossed silver casket belonging to Queen Isabel, which she may have used either as a jewel case or a reliquary. Tradition has it that it was from this very coffer that she took the jewels to finance Christopher Columbus' expedition to the New World. What is certain is that Isabel pawned her jewels on two other occasions to a bank belonging to the Santangels, a family of Jewish converts to the Christian faith who were close to the throne and had partly financed the war against the kingdom of Granada.

Above and opposite, the catafalques of King Phillip the Fair and Queen Joan by Bartolomé Ordoñez.

A second sepulchre belongs to the parents of the Emperor Charles V, Philip the Fair, son of the Emperor Maximillian, and his wife Queen Joan, eldest daughter of the Catholic King and Queen. It is somewhat higher than that of the Catholic Monarchs, composed as it is of two separate, superimposed sections with a funerary urn above these, upon which lie the recumbent figures of the king and queen. It was sculpted by Bartolomé Ordoñez, from Burgos, who is accepted as being one of the four great masters of the Spanish Renaissance style, although he worked mainly in Naples in collaboration at one time with his friend and fellow townsman Diego de Siloë. He also knew and was familiar with the work of Fanacelli, whose style he imitated to a large degree in this mausoleum, possibly following one of his earlier designs, although the sculpture of the figures on this tomb are more lifelike, showing an innate vigour in their forms which betrays much more the influence of Michael Angelo, whom he must have met in Carraras. The figure of St. Andrew represents a clear allusion and homage to Michael Angelo's Moses, and hints of the Greek Laocoön can be seen in the elaborately contorted figures adorning the front corners of the moulding on the lower part of the tomb. The magnificent anatomical detail of the nude mythological figures and the wealth of angels reminiscent of classical art are also more in the style of Michael Angelo, although the female forms are much more feminine than those sculpted by Michael Angelo himself, and the whole scene is filled with angels reminiscent of the fauns of classical art. The figures of the king and queen are idealised, above all that of Phillip the Fair, who had died sixteen years before but whose protruding Hapsburg chin, although not evident here, was well known

to his contemporaries. The figure of Queen Joan, although possibly not an exact likeness, bears similarities to her appearance when she was younger -she died thirty-five years after the mausoleum was built. The composure of the faces of the king and queen, softened by the texture of the marble, and their bodies, much more richly robed than those of the Catholic Monarchs, contrast with the great vitality which Ordoñez lent to the rest of the figures, which are sculpted in the purest Italian classical style, making the whole an outstanding example of the Italian Renaissance of the "cinquecento".

On the sides of the catafalque are delightful medallions containing scenes of the Birth of Christ, the Adoration of the Magi, Christ praying in the Garden of Gethsemane and the Descent from the Cross. The allegory of the Virtues and other symbolic figures occupy twelve small niches, which, according to Pita Andrade, "... together make up a strikingly vital group.". Unfortunately they made little or no impression upon Spanish sculpture of the time because although they arrived in Granada in 1539 they were not placed in the chapel until 1603.

The whole funereal emphasis of the Royal Chapel centres upon the main altarpiece, the architecture and sculptures of which complete its iconographic scheme, wholly devoted to the political and religious significance of the monarchy. On the upper pediment, figures of God the Father together with the Holy Ghost crown the great crucifix, which forms the nexus of the composition, surrounded by scenes of the Passion and the martyrdom of the patron saints of the chapel, St. John the Baptist and St. John the Evangelist. Although the work as a whole is attributed to the Burgundian Phillipe de Vigamy, it is very possible that Jacopo Florentino and Berruguete also had a hand in its design. Just like the chapel itself, the Plateresque retable was conceived at a crossroad of times, styles and ideologies. For the first time in an altar piece of this sort Renaissance elements, such as balusters, friezes decorated with small figures, semi-circular arches, sconces and grotesques were used. Instead of paintings, only very expressive, almost life-sized, fully rounded figures are to be seen. And the third contribution to Spanish altar-piece design lies in its physical layout and structure. It is divided according to the new order of things into horizontal levels and vertical sections, with a pediment flanked by semicircular arches and caissons containing statuettes on either side. On the springer of the arch are depicted the four scenes (shown here to the right and above) representing the baptism of the Muslim converts and the surrender of the city of Granada, authentic news reporting of the day.

To the left is what is thought to be a portrait of Charles V, and on the opposite page the high altar after the restoration of the whole funerary ensemble in the year 2000.

On show in the sacristy there are various personal possessions of considerable historical value, such as the gilded silver crown and sceptre of Queen Isabel and the gold-hilted sword of King Ferdinand, the reliquary of the queen, a collection of liturgical robes and the altar she carried with her on her campaigns against the Moors. Most impressive, however, for their intrinsic value, is Queen Isabel's private collection of Flemish paintings, which, although severely deteriorated, are considered to be the earliest collection of Flemish primitives, whose influence was to make an indelible impression on Spanish art. Her father, King John II of Castilla, was a great devotee of this new style of painting and it is recorded that Johan van Eyck stayed at King Johm's court on his way to Portugal.

Commercial relations between Castilla and Flanders based on the wool trade explain why the most outstanding civil portrait of the time, that of the merchant Amolfini and his wife, should have found its way to London via Ávila. The marriage of Queen Joan to Phillip the Fair increased the flow of these painted panels from Flanders to Spain and many of them, such as the Descent from the Cross by van der Weyden, hang today in the Prado museum. A magnificent copy of this painting can be seen in the transept of the Royal Chapel here in Granada. **Rogier van der Weyden** was born in Tournai in 1400 and together with van Eyck was one of the principal innovators of the new style. He seems to have been a student of Robert Campin, the Master of Flemale, from whom he learnt his love of humdrum daily subjects. But van der Weyden's mastery raises the conventional through transcendent symbolism to a much higher more personal level. He succeeds in transforming the objective, physical world into subjective emotion and intimate self-communion. He superseded his master's skills, even in the former's most original contribution to the new art, the depiction of clothing and drapery, and from van Eyck he learnt to combine the details of these new trends in a way that far surpassed the

AT THE BEGINNING OF THE XV CENTURY TWO COMPLETELY NEW SCHOOLS OF THOUGHT REVOLUTIONISED THE WORLD OF PAINTING IN COMPLETELY DIFFERENT WAYS: THE FLEMISH SCHOOL AND THE FLORENTINE SCHOOL. THE INFLUENCE OF BOTH SCHOOLS WAS WIDESPREAD UNTIL THE XIX CENTURY; IT CAN BE SAID THAT RATHER THAN THE END OF THE GOTHIC THEY REPRESENTED THE BEGINNING OF THE MODERN AGE IN ART.

TO THE ITALIAN SCHOOL SPACE WAS LIKE A INNATE REALITY WITH WHICH OBJECTS WERE IMBUED. THE RENAISSANCE, JUST LIKE THE GOTHIC, WAS ALSO CONCERNED WITH NATURALISM, BUT ABOVE ALL FROM A SCIENTIFIC POINT OF VIEW. THEY RECORDED AND ANALYSED EMPIRICAL DATA. THEIR PAINTING HAS AN INTANGIBLE QUALITY; IT IS AN ART OF LINES AND EDGES. THE FLEMISH SCHOOL, THROUGH VAN EYCK, EMBARKED UPON A DIFFERENT ROAD. THEY ACHIEVED THE ILLUSION OF NATURALNESS BY PATIENTLY ADDING ONE DETAIL AFTER ANOTHER UNTIL THEY MANAGED TO TURN THE PAINTING INTO A KIND OF MIRROR OF THE VISIBLE WORLD. PERSPECTIVE, INSTEAD OF BEING BASED UPON FORM AND PROPORTION, WAS RELEGATED TO FULFILLING THE SECONDARY TECHNICAL ROLE OF UNIFYING THE WHOLE. THE STRUCTURE IS SURROUNDED BY A SPACE WHICH IS INTANGIBLE, IMMATERIAL AND INFINITE BUT EVER PRESENT, AND SEEMS TO EMANATE FROM OBJECTS AND EXPAND FOR EVER. SPACE DID NOT DETERMINE SHAPES NOR DID IT FRAME THE PROPORTIONS DELIMITING THESE SHAPES; IT WAS RATHER SOMETHING AETHERIAL ENVELOPING EVERYTHING. THIS SPACE IS TINGED WITH THE LIGHT THAT GIVES REALITY TO THE SHAPES AND OBJECTS FROM WHICH IT APPEARS TO DIFFUSE.

TO ACHIEVE THIS NEW REALITY PAINTING WITH OILS HAD TO BE REINVENTED. UNTIL THIS TIME THE USUAL MEDIUM OF PAINTING HAD BEEN TEMPERA, BASED ON A MIXTURE OF VEGETABLE PIGMENTS AND GROUND-UP MINERALS TO WHICH EGG YOLK WAS ADDED TO FORM A PASTE. THIS MIXTURE WAS WONT TO DRY RAPIDLY AND SO VAN EYCK REPLACED THE EGG YOLK WITH A DRYING OIL MIXED WITH SOME OTHER UNKNOWN SUBSTANCE THAT WAS SOLUBLE IN OIL WITHOUT PRODUCING AN EMULSION. THE NEW FORMULA DRIED MUCH MORE SLOWLY AND SO ALLOWED HIM TO MANUFACTURE TRANSPARENT COLOURS THAT COULD BE APPLIED ONE COAT AT A TIME, SUPERIMPOSING GLAZES TO ACHIEVE THE MORE LUMINOUS FEATURES. IN THE SAME WAY THE COLOURS WERE MUCH MORE VIVID THAN ANY KNOWN UP TO THAT TIME, ALLOWING THE LIGHT TO REFLECT FROM A SMOOTH, OPAQUE SURFACE. WHAT IS MORE, HE COULD USE MUCH FINER HORSE-HAIR OR PIG-BRISTLE BRUSHES AND OPTICAL DEVICES TO HELP WITH THE WORK. A CLEAR RELATIONSHIP EXISTS BETWEEN THE TECHNIQUES USED AND THE ARTIST'S INTENTIONS. ONLY OIL PAINTING ALLOWS THE ARTIST TO REPRODUCE THE ATMOSPHERE AND EFFECTS OF THE LIGHT, RELATIONSHIPS THAT BIND THE INFINITELY SMALL TO THE UNIVERSE AS A WHOLE, THE MEANS TO WELD TOGETHER THE INTERIOR AND EXTERIOR SPACE IN THE PAINTING.

THE NEW FLEMISH REALISM ALSO DEVELOPED A HIDDEN SYMBOLISM ACCORDING TO WHICH MUNDANE OBJECTS ARE IMBUED WITH SYMBOLIC MEANINGS DISGUISED BENEATH DECEPTIVE VISIBLE APPEARANCES.

mere accumulation of objects, relating solid objects one to another and thus opening and emphasising the surrounding spaces. There are two other magnificent panels in the Royal Chapel: a Descent from the Cross and a Nativity, both belonging to a triptych, the third panel of which is in New York.

These works are very typical of the Flemish master, who was responsible for the greatest impact on European art in his day. In the Descent from the Cross the suffering is exquisitely restrained at all levels, with no recourse to any excess of tone or gesture. The painter's use of colour and draughtsmanship are a re-flection of his own emotions. The range of colours is sparse, hardly distinguishing the various solid forms and blurring the reliefs, but at the same time expressing in minute detail the shape of the nose, eyebrows, lips and every facial contour. In the Nativity, the Virgin Mary's hands are elegant and aristocratic, slightly softened by

the chiaroscuro that gives form to the details as they emerge gradually into the light. His textures, especially those of the skin, are one of his finest achievements. His settings are vague and indeterminate, with no special allusions to form, so that nothing might distract the attention away from the scene in the foreground. But they always provide it with a true and harmonious frame.

Dierick Bouts was born in Haarlem in 1415 and was the first great Dutch painter to make his mark upon the important school of painting that flourished in the north of Europe at the time. He borrowed his approach to light from van Eyck, and from van Weyden his subjects and elegant models; he imbued his work with all his predecessors' skills but went on to create his own special aesthetic style in developing the subjects he most admired in very original ways. He is considered a worthy heir to van Eyck,

the link between the first generation of Dutch masters and later generations, who referred to Bouts as "the inventor of landscape" because of his acutely developed sense of space and the relationship that exists between figures and the landscape, which he strips of all unnecessary adornment to integrate it thus into his own austere, mystical and profoundly religious world. He accentuates the stature of the figures by elongating their torsos, and in order to heighten their expression often shows them in profile. His forms are geometric and his organisation of scenery rational, even with a hint of engineering behind them, but despite this, in his overall design he achieves a sense of perfect naturalness, which marks an important improvement on the technique of van Eyck. Nobody before Bouts had managed to portray such stirring and dramatic twilights, to capture the essence of the seasons, depict tortuous rocky crags and reflect the moods of the weather so justly. One of his most outstanding works is the triptych of the Passion that now hangs in the sacristy (above) and the portrait of Christ, whose deep and disturbing, but at the same time majestically serene gaze radiates a profound sense of being beyond human understanding.

Hans Memling was born in Aschaffenbourg in Germany around 1430. He received his early training as a painter in Cologne although it was not until he had served his apprenticeship in Van der Weyden's workshop that he reached maturity and achieved recognition by contemporary middle class society, for whom he painted what are considered to be some of the finest portraits of all time. His diptych of the Descent from the Cross, the Pietà and the Virgin and Child preserve the mysticism and delicate compositional features learned from his master, together with a minute detail of the landscape, whilst at the same time offering a magisterial study of the serene countenance and velvet texture of the clothing.

Above, the Descent from the Cross by Van der Weyden, and below, Prayer in the Garden of Gethsemane by Boticelli. On the following pages, details from paintings by Hans Memling

The Cathedral

Capilla Real

The Church of the Holy Shrine (built upon the erstwhile Muslim mosque).

On the previous page: A view of the inside of the cathedral from the main chapel in which can be seen a gradual slimming of the bulk of the stone within the main arch as it rises upwards towards the keystone in order to maintain the concave, cylindrical shape, despite displacing somewhat the centre of gravity.

THE CATHEDRAL

Plans for the Cathedral were drawn up at the same time as those for the Royal Chapel. It was designed to be the episcopal centre, the symbolic monument to put the seal on the Christian conquest, the hub and point of reference of the new faith and new reality that would point the way along the social path to be followed in the centuries to come. Nevertheless, work was not begun until 1523, under the direction of the old masters of the Gothic, Enrique Egas and Juan Gil de Hontañón, who merely repeated well-worn schemes from their earlier designs.

During his honeymoon and state visit to Granada in 1526 Charles V decided to convert the cathedral into the pantheon for his dynasty, which speeded up the work in hand somewhat. The real impulse however came with the arrival from Burgos of a young architect of Flemish origin, Diego de Siloë, who joined the project in 1528 and immediately made radical changes to the design, offering Renaissance ideas, which affected both its architectural shape and ideological content. Initially the emperor was not at all sure about de Siloë's plans, worried that the new ideas may detract from

the original design of the Royal Chapel, so de Siloë had to go to Toledo to convince his Emperor, with the support of archbishop Fonseca, that the new style was fitting and more appropriate for a Caesar. It would be rooted in traditional Christianity, the main chapel, intended to be the pantheon of the Habsburgs, being built in the form of a completely independent round tower with an ambulatory, reminiscent of the Church of the Holy Sepulchre in Jerusalem. It is entered from the transept via an imperial triumphal arch in such a way that this layout sprang both from early Christian buildings and also from the Romanesque tradition, for it must be remembered that Charles V was Emperor of the Holy Roman-Germanic empire and so was heir to both traditions. The result of this new way of approaching the concept of space, created upon the basis of vast spaces and a double transept with soaring naves, was a regal processional church, only about a third of which is visible from the main chapel. For the next 35 years Diego de Siloë devoted himself to building one of the most significant monuments of universal art.

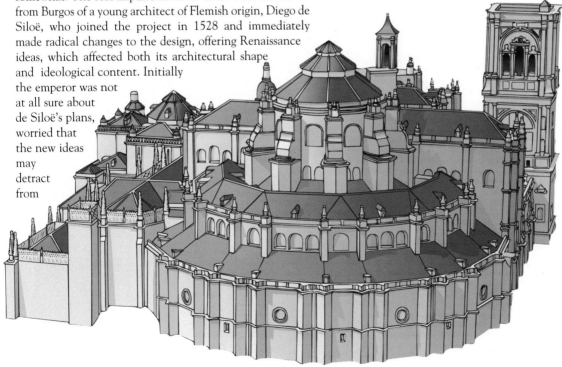

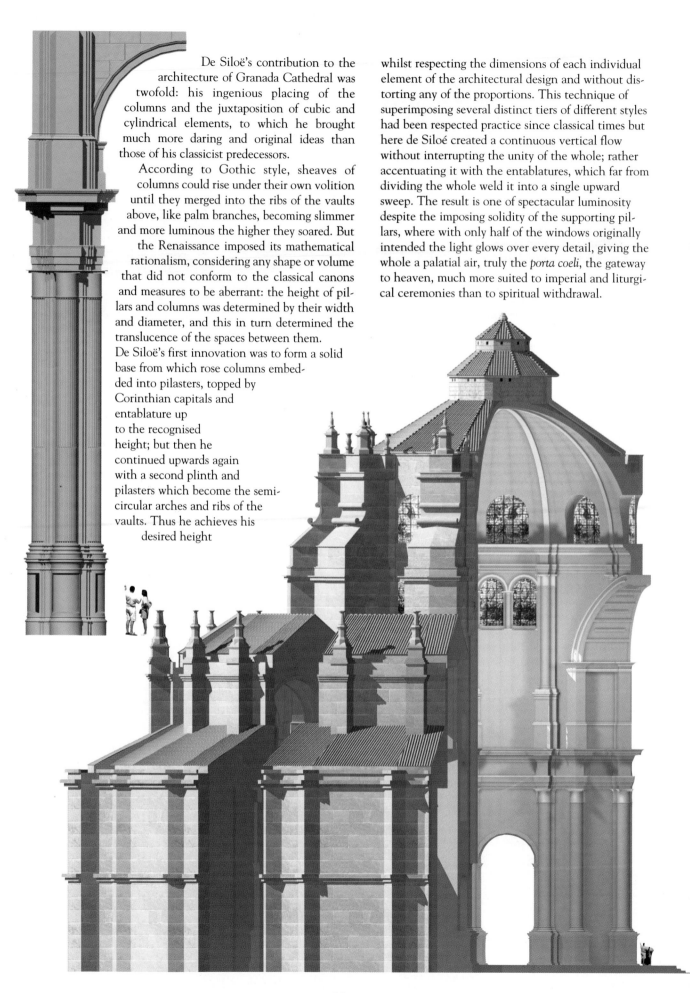

De Siloë's contribution to the architecture of Granada Cathedral was twofold: his ingenious placing of the columns and the juxtaposition of cubic and cylindrical elements, to which he brought much more daring and original ideas than those of his classicist predecessors.

According to Gothic style, sheaves of columns could rise under their own volition until they merged into the ribs of the vaults above, like palm branches, becoming slimmer and more luminous the higher they soared. But the Renaissance imposed its mathematical rationalism, considering any shape or volume that did not conform to the classical canons and measures to be aberrant: the height of pillars and columns was determined by their width and diameter, and this in turn determined the translucence of the spaces between them. De Siloë's first innovation was to form a solid base from which rose columns embedded into pilasters, topped by Corinthian capitals and entablature up to the recognised height; but then he continued upwards again with a second plinth and pilasters which become the semicircular arches and ribs of the vaults. Thus he achieves his desired height

whilst respecting the dimensions of each individual element of the architectural design and without distorting any of the proportions. This technique of superimposing several distinct tiers of different styles had been respected practice since classical times but here de Siloé created a continuous vertical flow without interrupting the unity of the whole; rather accentuating it with the entablatures, which far from dividing the whole weld it into a single upward sweep. The result is one of spectacular luminosity despite the imposing solidity of the supporting pillars, where with only half of the windows originally intended the light glows over every detail, giving the whole a palatial air, truly the *porta coeli*, the gateway to heaven, much more suited to imperial and liturgical ceremonies than to spiritual withdrawal.

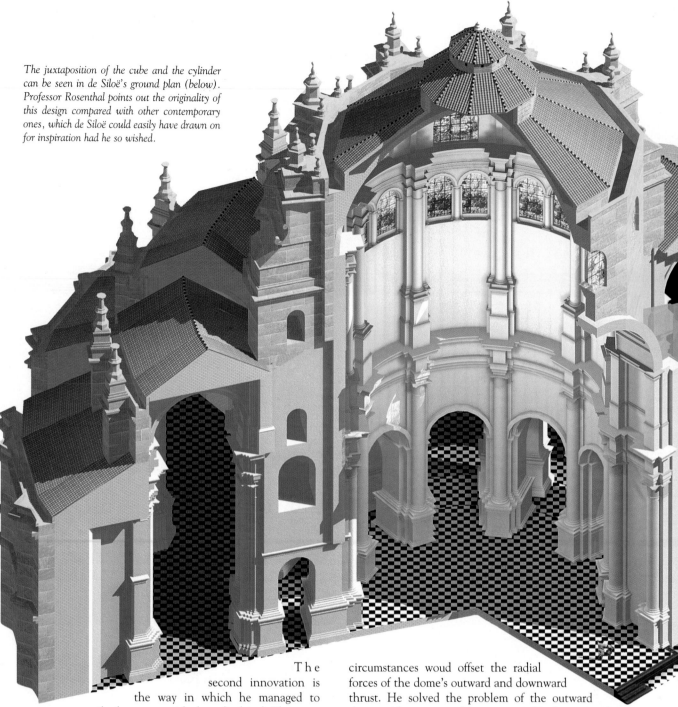

The juxtaposition of the cube and the cylinder can be seen in de Siloë's ground plan (below). Professor Rosenthal points out the originality of this design compared with other contemporary ones, which de Siloë could easily have drawn on for inspiration had he so wished.

The second innovation is the way in which he managed to reconcile the square with the cylindrical. The superimposition of both shapes was a permanent challenge for Renaissance architects but had its precedents in the Church of the Annunciation and the Cathedral in Florence, where de Siloë had served his apprenticeship. In most cases the weight of the dome was spread among its supporting pillars throughout an entire circle (Look, for example at St. Peter's Basilica in Rome and the constructions of Bramante and Alberti.). In Granada, de Siloë, following a rough draft by Bramante, proposed a novel solution to the problem by juxtaposing rather than joining both individual elements (a cube and a cylinder rising fifteen metres above it) by means of a triumphal arch which would have to support more than a third of the entire weight of the enormous dome, 45 metres high and 20 metres in diameter. Both elements being independent, the arch would not be provided with the counterweight of the rectangular naves which in normal circumstances woud offset the radial forces of the dome's outward and downward thrust. He solved the problem of the outward thrust with enormous buttresses, visible from outside, but inside the whole weight had to be adsorbed by the keystone of the triumphal arch. This ingenious solution was not a product of whim but born of the need to create a circular main chapel, a central space which was at one and the same time open and a focal point, very different from the disperse Gothic sanctuaries and also from the rest of the cathedral because it was designed to hold the royal tombs, a space intended to resemble the Church of the Holy Sepulchre in Jerusalem, which tradition held to be circular. In the words of Professor Sánchez Mesa, "In this great humanist temple a harmonious tension is achieved between the sacred and the profane, between the static solidity of the buttresses and the slender agility of the structure itself, rhythmically open to the outside, with stained-glass windows which turn the sanctuary into a huge pyramidal lantern, filled with monumental symbolism, unity and harmony.".

The whole ceiling of the central nave can be seen in the photograph on the right, taken from directly below. The main chapel (right) is covered with a Renaissance splayed vault whilst the rest of the vaults, including those of the transept, are Gothic and therefore already unfashionable by the XVI century. In fact, it would seem that the masons were incapable of carrying out de Siloë's original design and chose to take the easy way out by using ribbed vaulting, which, having been the mainstay of vaulting throughout the middle ages, they would have been very familiar with.

CATEDRAL

0 5 10 15 20 25 30M

The light filters into the main chapel through stained-glass windows, which endow it with vividly contrasting hues, creating on high an atmosphere of colourful lucidity and turning the cupola into a symbol of Domus Dei et Porta Coeli, the House of God and the Gateway to Heaven. These windows are designed to be looked at from a distance of at least fifty metres but when examined closely it can be

rocks, clouds and columns. This is in fact very difficult to achieve in stained glass, where it is the light itself which should contribute the third dimension of perspective. The first level of stained glass, depicting the life of Jesus, is set in double windows at the sides, occupying the entire span of the arches, whilst those above, occupying twice the area of the former, represent his passion and death.

seen that each image is constructed as painstakingly as though it were a painted portrait. Apart from the anatomical perfection of the human figures, the measure and reference point of all proportions in the Renaissance, there is a clear desire to create perspective by using pictorial devices such as

Pita Andrade comments that the area of the main chapel opens onto the main body of the church whilst at the same time remaining confined within the great cylinder covered by the hemisphere of the cupola. Within this space, clearly divided into two architectural elements, we see the development of the iconographic narrative that explains the whole ensemble. At the first level the splayed arches remain obscure, in the darkest part of the cathedral, bound to the earth, like mankind confined to the murky shadows. At the second level, the vault with its radial ribbing rests upon columns embedded into pilasters, hiding the huge buttresses, between which run wide windows and paintings to transform their weight into light. Here are recounted the mysteries and the life of Jesus. The diffuse light filtering through the stained glass is the light of glory and redemption, which can only be attained through the Virgin Mary whose life is shown here in the paintings of Carlos Cano) and by the virtue of the Passion of Christ. It represents the synthesis of important theological concepts, captured within the confines of this sanctuary, a pragmatic approach to make religious teaching manifest here on earth, an attempt to reconcile Platonism with the Church, reason with faith. Originally it was intended that all the windows of the cathedral should contain stained glass but this enterprise was never completed. The most finished and significant are those belonging to the main chapel above). The lower ones were made by Theodor van Holland and comprise 14

panes representing scenes from the life of Jesus. They betray clear signs of both Italian and Flemish influence which might be expected from an artist who, although born in Amsterdam, lived in Ambères and served his apprenticeship in Italy. The higher frieze of windows, the theme of which incorporates the Passion and Death of Christ, is the work of the Dutchman Johan van Kamp, who was also an architect and sculptor. He is known to have made the panes in Granada and was thus probably very aware of the intentions of de Siloë, who almost certainly contributed to their design, as may be seen in the "monumentality and volume, and the vitality incorporated into the figures" (Victor Nieto). As far as Pita Andrade is concerned, "The stained-glass windows represent the most important collection of their kind in the Spanish Renaissance and the final vibrant expression of this art until our own times.". Beneath the windows, between the light and the shadows, are a series of paintings on canvas by Alonso Cano which allude to the life of the Virgin Mary, and have also been referred to as "unique in the history of Spanish painting". Alonso Cano was a painter, architect and sculptor of the Baroque school, who allowed himself to be guided by his devotion to the classicism of Michael Angelo, so creating a style proper to the Baroque in his shapes whilst majestically classicist in his backgrounds He resorts to optical devices in his paintings such as stairways

plinths, grilles and other architectural elements, in order to create differences in the perspective of surroundings, volumes and scenery. To achieve this Cano always took into account the quallity of the light, the situation, and above all, the frame of reference of his paintings, in such a way that his work harmonises to perfection with the rest of the elements in the main chapel. This harmony is precisely the great achievement of the design as a whole. The volume of the clothing, emphasised by the reds and blues so typical of Cano, contrast with the sweet delicacy of the Virgin's face, which, without losing the classical sense of serenity, gives her a gentleness impossible to find in classical Romanesque matrons and goddesses.

In the small sculpture of the Immaculate Conception of the Sacristy (*right*) the delicate hands and the distant gaze mark the distance between the human and the divine, in the style of Fidias; she represents the beatitude of the Mother of God untouched by original sin.

SYNBOLISM: Works of art serve to help us understand the moment in history in which they were made and the way in which their makers thought. During the Renaissance, man stood erect in the centre of a geocentric universe, considering himself to be the universal measure and canon, made in the likeness of God, and thus human art is a reflection of divinity. His own self-confidence distances him from Romanesque mysticism, and Gothic naturalism surrenders him to a certain kind of pagan rational-ism, turn-ing towards the ancient world that he considers himself to be heir to. Just over four thousand years had passed in the history of the earth since the creation of man and after centuries of darkness the faith of Jesus Christ would be imposed on mankind. The holiness of space becomes wide, limitless and powerful, almost overwhelming, a space in which man, its creator, feels small but at the same time close to heaven. Granada Cathedral, the house of God and the Emperor, is a good example in which the construction, in the name of ideas, explains the historical moment through which the Spanish monarchy was passing. Upon the great pillars supporting the main arch, which would form the focus of the worshipers' attention, appear the figures of Adam (*above left*) and Eve (*right*), the father and mother of all human kind, and some few feet directly below them, at prayer, the Catholic King and Queen, their heirs and successors, defenders of the faith, all represent-ing a manifestation of firm beliefs admitting no room for doubt, the conviction that they would carry the light of the gospel throughout the world.

PUERTA DEL PERDON

The great Renaissance masters were trained in all aspects of the arts and were ready to take on any of the tasks required to bring their projects to conclusion. Documents of the time describe them attired in the aprons of their guilds and pitching in with the work. De Siloë drew and designed for the workshops and even sculpted some of the figures that form an integral part of his architectural scheme.

La Puerta del Perdón (*the door of Forgiveness, right*) provides entrance to the main nave and is at the same time the doorway to the Royal Chapel, as the original doorway to the chapel was finally enclosed within the cathedral itself. Thus the ornamental motifs refer to both churches and belong equally to the Catholic Monarchs and their grandson Charles V, whose shields cover the surrounding buttresses. It forms a monumental doorway-cum-ornamental screen, "wherein is achieved the happiest of balances between the architectural and the sculptural", and a suitable foretaste of what awaits within the cathedral itself. It is composed of three different architectural sections of which only the first was worked upon by de Siloë. This is in the form of a triumphal arch, above which recline the figures of Faith and Justice, bearing a plaque announcing the conquest and vindicating the Christian enterprise after seven hundred years of Muslim rule. A proliferation of Plateresque adornment accentuates the chiaroscuro of the niches and the bulk of the salient reliefs. The concept and design of this doorway constituted an example for de Siloë's disciples to follow for generations to come, and its influence was still to be seen in the late Baroque of the XVIII century.

De Siloë's original designs for the façade remains unknown, the wooden model he made of it having been lost, but there are accounts which mention a huge portal with three triumphal Roman arches leading into the five interior naves, framed by twin towers, which would weld it into a harmonious whole. Only one of the towers was eventually built, and that incompletely.

Alonso Cano, who so faithfully interpreted de Siloé's intentions and style, designed the façade that we see today in the year of his own death (1667). According to experts on the subject, a hundred years after de Siloé outlined his original scheme, Cano kept as close as to this original project as he could, at least as far as the basic design is concerned, but Cano was an architect who lived in the Baroque and could never really detach himself from the classical mould, above all from the Manneristic period (initi-

ated by Michael Angelo), from which he drew his ideas to break what for him represented the overly rigid norms of classicism by introducing new forms of adornment and innovative structural rhythms. Cano's Baroque style is more evident in the superficial details and forms than in the basic structure; he replaced capitals with medallions and floral motifs, used pilasters wherever possible instead of columns, and accentuated the chiaroscuro by pushing the walls between them into the background. He also scattered around figures of apostles and evangelists, which is in complete discord with Baroque rhetoric, even though the sculpting of the figures themselves falls within its canon. His construction in the end was one where the voluminous bulk of the structure and its large-scale finials dominate the decoration, which in itself is much more restrained than that of the entrance, the Door of Forgiveness.

Throughout the ages Granada has been dreamed of by travellers, nurturing fantastic images of an oriental paradise in the south of Europe. But after the Christian conquest history did not cease to flow in Granada; it became the hub of a new dynamic age in all the arts, the focal point of the latest fashions and innovations, all of which resulted in the creation of the richest and most complete group of monuments ever conceived during the period from the Renaissance to the Baroque. Any other city able to boast of such a heritage of Western art would be ranked among the most important in Europe, but the attraction of the Alhambra has always overshadowed everything which grew up around it, much of which remains undiscovered today by many visitors to the city. This phenomenon is added to by a certain lack of interest among its own population, who tend to look somewhat askance at tourism. In 2000 a tourist voucher was introduced, the intention being to encourage and facilitate a wider knowledge of Granada's historical-cultural heritage, including routes to walk around the city, which on their own merit alone would

Bono Turístico

fully justify a visit. The voucher includes visits to the three best known monuments: the Alhambra, the Royal Chapel and the Cathedral, which at a rush might be visited during one day, and also the Carthusian Monastery and that of St. Jerome, wonderful examples of Andalucian and Renaissance Baroque respectively. Apart from this, the voucher allows admission to the museums of Archeology and Fine Arts and to the modern Science Park on the outskirts of the city. These visits take you on fairly short walks through the historical centre of the city, along the course of the river Darro, part of which has long since been vaulted over to allow traffic to flow through the town. Just beside the Cathedral and opposite the Royal Chapel is the Madraza, the Muslim university founded in the XIV century by the Sultan Yusuf I, which also contains the remains of a restored mosque. The Alcaicería, the Muslim silk market, burnt to the ground in the XIX

Above is a view of the Cathedral from the Parque del Triunfo. Below that, the symbol to be found on the tourist voucher. To the left is a view of the Plaza de Isabel la Católica by night. To the right, a view of the cupola of the Madraza, the original medieval Muslim university. On the opposite page, a view from the Hotel Luz (above) and some details of the Alcaicería, the old Muslim silk market (below).

Plaza de Isabel
la Católica

century, is today a rebuilt labyrinth of narrow streets and small shops with all the air of a medieval souk, which leads out on one side into Zacatín street, where clothes were sold in Muslim times, and on the other into the Plaza de Bib Rambla, which in times gone by used to be the real city centre and is today the site of flower stalls and pleasant pavement cafés. This square is overlooked by the Archbishop's Palace, which was the original seat of the Christian University of Granada when it was founded by the Emperor Charles V on his state visit to Granada in 1526, during his honey-moon with Isabel of Portugal, the most beautiful woman in Europe. Just to the south of this square, across the main thoroughfare, Reyes Católicos street, is the town hall, housed in what used to be a Carmelite convent. At the lower corner of the square in front of it is Navas street, full of taverns and wine-bars, where Granadans go to stroll and enjoy a drink and a snack (tapa). Behind the town hall, along Mariana Pineda

Corral del Carbón

street, which runs parallel to Reyes Católicos street, is the Corral de Carbón (left and below), the only Moorish *caravansera*, or *fundak*, to have survived to our times. These were overnight stopping places for mule drivers and their trains, and in the centre of the courtyard water still runs in the original drinking trough. The surrounding rooms were once stables but are now offices occupied by the tourist bureau. The rooms around the upper galleries house the offices of El Legado Andalusí, a scheme to introduce tourists to some of the old mule and pedestrian routes through Andalucía. Leaving the Corral de Carbón and returning to Reyes Católicos street the visitor will eventually come to the Plaza de Isabel la Católica, in the centre of which is a statue commemorating Queen Isabel's granting of patents to Christopher Columbus to leave on his expedition to the new world (above). Thence to Plaza Nueva, home of the Royal Chancellery, a magnificent XVI century Renaissance buil-

ding, and the church of St. Ana, with the silhouette of the watchtower of the Alhambra on the hill above it. From Plaza Nueva the narrow Carrera del Darro follows the course of the river between the old Muslim quarter of the Albaicín on the left and the steep scarp of the Alhambra towering over the opposite bank of the river on the right. A little way along are the remains of the XI century Muslim bridge known as the Puente del Cadí, or the Magistrate's Bridge, and just opposite on the left, el Bañuelo, one of the few remaining Arab baths in the city, also dating from the XI century. A couple of hundred yards farther on is the XVI century Church of St. Peter *(bottom left)* and the adjoining houses of Zafra and Castril *(bottom right)*, nowadays home to the Museums of Fine Arts and Archaeology respectively.

Finally the narrow street widens into the Paseo de los Tristes, a wide area of pavement cafés where one can sit and admire the majesty of the Alhambra Palace looming from the crest of the red hill just above. From here an unmetalled track, the Cuesta de los Chinos, winds up to the Alhambra and the Generalife, having first skirted a new construction, el Rey Chico, the building permission of which is undoubtedly one of the greatest political offences perpetrated on the aesthetics of the city in its recent history. In the opposite direction, to the left, the Cuesta del Chapiz climbs up between the hills of the Albaicín and the Sacromonte.

Southern façades in Plaza Nueva and the Church of St. Ana with the watchtower of the citadel of the Alhambra above.

Above, the Royal Chancellery. Below left, the Carrera del Darro with the Casa de Zafra on the left and the Church of St. Peter in the background. Right, the Casa de Castril.

Visitors often declare that Granada is one of the most beautiful cities in Spain, not just for its historical and cultural heritage but also because of its setting, its general atmosphere, and famous quarters such as the Albaicín. But there are other less well known neighbourhoods that share the same essential beauties endowed upon them by centuries of history which a visitor should see to gain a really intimate impression of the city. The Realejo, for example, the old Jewish quarter lying at the foot of the Mauror hill, the southern slope of the red hill of the Alhambra, is centred around a square of great character and charm, the Campo del Principe. What was not so long ago an open field is now a square planted with trees, a meeting place for local residents and visitors alike, who come here to sit at one of the many outdoor terraces of the bars and cafés around the square, while the kids kick a football around away from the danger of the traffic (above). From here one can look upwards and see among the cypress trees the white cubic lines of the modernist town house and fine-arts foundation built by the Rodríguez Acosta family. Within a couple of minutes' walk from the Campo del Principe are several buildings worth visiting, such as the Casa de los Tiros, and the Cuarto Real de Santo Domingo a Muslim palace. To return to the city centre it is worth taking a

slightly roundabout way, walking south-westward downhill to arrive at the Paseo del Salón, an avenue which runs along the banks of the river Genil, and from there upwards again along the avenue of the Virgen de las Angustias, the patron Virgin of Granada, past the church devoted to her, and on to what is nowadays the true heart of the city, Puerta Real (The Royal Gate), with its newly planted pomegranate tree, the symbol of Granada. If, standing here, a visitor can imagine that only a few years ago this spot was no more than half a mile from the open spaces of the great fertile plain which extends westwards from the city, he will realise what a tightly knit city Granada really is and that most of its architectural glories are in short walking distance of each other: streets such as San Juan de Dios (St. John of God, the founder of the Hospitaliers) with its church and hospital dedicated to the XVI century Granadan saint, the Church of St. Justo and St. Pastor, the XVII century Faculty of Law and the College of Pharmacy (left). And for those who enjoy the bustle of the market place, the meat and fish market, St. Agustín, just below the Gran Vía de Colón.. All in all there are so many hidden corners and backwaters to discover in old Granada that a visitor on foot can happily fill many days of continuous surprises and subtle delights.

Paseo del Salón

The modern sports centre, built to include the latest technological developments. A large part of the public seating will fold away to allow full use of the complex for a multitude of different types of event.

The International Congress Centre offers an ideal venue for meetings and conferences in a modern setting. (Below) The Science Park has been such a highly successful initiative that many other Spanish cities are intent on emulating it. Qualified attendants explain scientific principles to visitors in a practical and easily understandable way. It has recently been extended to include the Centre for Environmental Studies.

Parque de las Ciencias

Professor Arturo Gutierrez Castillo has devoted many years to the study of this hill, the oldest settlement and most legendary quarter in the whole of Granada, and describes it thus:

Above, the mirador of St. Nicholas, offering a panoramic view of the Alhambra, which changes constantly in beauty and magficence according to the hour of the day or night.

Above, la Casa Arabe, a well-known house in the Albaicín, retaining many original aspects of a Nasrid dwelling despite having been restored.

The Albaicín is a place of wonder, oozing with the essence of centuries gone by, where history moves discernibly and unashamedly. This is as it should be: the inexhaustible legacy of ancient civilisations, the hoary witness who has survived the ravages of time and tide, and a sentimental refuge for romantic, nostalgic souls. But it may be that trying to define it in this way means little or nothing to those who have never had the chance to discover the place and get to know it. That's the risk inherent in words, for no matter how hard one might try to choose them they are never quite so precise or accurate as they were intended to be. Above all when they presume to explain the inexplicable. This brief allusion to the limits that language imposes is nothing more than an excuse for writing about the Albaicín in the traditional descriptive way, best fitting for someone who has never heard of it nor seen it before, referring endlessly to the seductive charms that have made it justly famous as the most intriguing and exotic quarter in the whole of Granada. For example, its houses jumbled one on top of another like swallows' nests, its inexplicably twisting, narrow streets and alleys, the profusion of flowers and greenery drooping over the walls of its houses and orchards, the sudden, breath-taking views of the Alhambra, the Sierra Nevada and the plain away to the west, the secret corners which suddenly appear and offer themselves to the eyes of the lucky

Above, Plaza Larga decorated for the Day of the Cross. Below, a typical square in the Albaicín.

The first of these photographs was taken in the 1950's and the second fifty years later, clearly schowing the steady decline of the Sacromonte during the last half century

Above, the street market in Plaza Larga. Below, the Church of St. Bartholomew.

Of Granada´s many mosques during the days of Muslim rule all that remains is this courtyard (below) in the Church of San Salvador.

persistent traveller... And for those who want something more, because they are not content with the pleasures of the senses alone, there is also history and art all around them.

Mixed in with the houses, even forming part of them at times, there are vestiges of history that take this quarter back to the earliest cultures and civilisations known in Spain, peoples whose history has sometimes been overshadowed by the glory of the Muslim period in Granada. And in fact this would seem to be the destiny of this quarter: the constant evocation of the times which gave it its maximum splendour. When at the beginning of the VIII century Asad ben Abderraman al Saybani ordered the construction of a fortress on what is now the Plaza de San Nicolás, the *qasabat Garnata*, according to Muslim chroniclers, he could never have imagined the future awaiting it. By the XI century it had become the site of the palatial residence of the first Islamic dynasty to rule these lands, the Zirids. Thus arose the citadel, *Alcazaba Cadima*, and in the protection of its shadow numerous small districts and quarters until the whole hill was occupied. It continued to prosper, even when in the XIII century Muhammad al Hamar decide to move his court to the Sabika hill on the other side of the river, which in time would become the imposing citadel of the Alhambra.

The Albaicín, true to its good fortune, continued to grow until it became a veritable city within the city of Granada. In the XIV century it had its own army, civil administration and magistracy; the Nasrid aristocracy built their sumptuous palaces and mansions on its hillsides; it could boast some thirty mosques, including a main mosque more elegant than that of the city of Granada itself; an ingeniously complex network of water mains fed cisterns in every quarter; the constant clacking of looms proclaimed the existence of a busy commerce in high quality cloths and silks; a multitude of wares of all kinds: leather, ceramic, enamel, glass, copper, wrought iron and marquetry in a myriad different forms flowed ceaselessly from the household workshops, expressing the inexhaustible imagination and limitless industrial drive of its population.

This was the Albaicín in its days of glory, admired and to some extent feared, because its population was not only numerous but also fractious and difficult to govern. And this is the legendary Albaicín which illogically we all want to see around us. Nowadays there is nothing left of that Albaicín except a few atavistic relics, rather traces of the past that have survived by mere chance after the arrival of the new Christian powers. We should not lament overly because of this; the designs of history are irrefutable in leaving everyone and everything in its place. Nor should there be room for complaint, for if History has turned its back on the Albaicín, Nature has tried to compensate. So today's Albaicín is perfumed with the springtime smells of walled gardens and enlivened with the colours of plants and flowers determined to escape the confines of their walls; sudden changes of scene from dark to light, like squares on a chess board and the inevitable panoramic views. From time to time the severity of a monastery wall or the elegance of a palatial mansion or the soaring spire of a bell tower or the twittering of sparrows in the branches overhead or the dis-

tant bark of a dog will remind us of the presence of a closer Albaicín of much more daily routine.

Any visit to the Albaicín should be made with no predetermined course in mind, no map in hand. The best guide is that which invites one to lose oneself and to improvise; that which suggests climbing to the highest point and then allowing oneself to descend through the narrow lanes until reaching level ground once more. That is the sincerest and truest way; the disinterested advice of a good friend. But one can't completely ignore the evidence of massed opinion, which elevates some places in the Albaicín to the category of "unmissable". And so, not to differ from the rest, we must pay homage to the enchantment of such places which seduce all those who see them: the miradors of San Nicolás and San Cristóbal, the squares of San Miguel Bajo and Plaza Larga, streets such as la Lona, Agua, las Caldererías, el Zenete, the square of los Carvajales and the Paseo de los Tristes ... because even when it is crowded the climb up to the Albaicín is always worth it."

THE MONASTERY OF SAN JERONIMO (ST. JEROME)

This monastery was founded by the Catholic Monarchs as one of the many building projects that they instigated immediately after the conquest in their desire to Christianise the city as quickly as possible, a task confided basically to the trust of the three great religious orders of the day: the Franciscans, the Dominicans and the Jeronymites. The monastery was placed in the keeping of this latter order, to which Queen Isabel's personal confessor, Fray Hernando de Talavera, belonged. It quickly became known for being a refuge for Jewish converts. Fray Hernando de Talavera, the first archbishop of Granada, combined humility with wisdom and was also a friend to the defeated Muslims. His conciliatory counsel, ignored by his successor Cardinal Cisneros, would without doubt have changed many of the darker consequences of the conquest.

The monastery was founded in 1492 but was not begun until 1504 and thus its initial architectural style was Gothic, with a typical convent church in the shape of a Latin cross with only one nave, side chapels and raised choir. Just one more church among many designed by an anonymous draughtsman, but which had the luck to be touched by the genius of de Siloë, who arrived in Granada in 1526 ostensibly to work on this monastery but obviously attracted by the cathedral project. First to be built was the great Gothic cloister with thirty-six semicircular arches, completed in 1519. The following year the finishing touches were put to the second, smaller cloister, named after the Empress Isabel, who stayed here during her honeymoon in 1526. The six porches on the first floor of the large cloister, clearly designed by de Siloë, confer a classical majesty upon the monastic simplicity of the earlier construction. These porches belonged to the private chapels of illustrious Granadan families and royal dependencies.

The building of the church, which began in 1519, passed into the hands of Jacomo Florentino el Indaco six years afterwards, having been ceded to the widow of the "Gran Capitan". But it was the arrival

on the scene of de Siloë two years later that gave a complete new vision to the work and turned the monastery into a first class Renaissance monument, changing the style while work was in progress without creating any lack of harmony, something which can be appreciated immediately by a glance at the large windows, sconces, shields and other decorative details both inside and out. On the main façade the difference is immediately clear between the workmanship of the upper window by de Siloë and the considerably inferior craftsmanship of the shield of the Catholic Monarchs below. De Siloë was also responsible for constructing the tower, which was destroyed by the French at the beginning of the XIX century and restored in 1916. But where his genius really shines through is in the transept, which was built by el Indaco in close collaboration with de Siloë, covered by an original groined vault in the shape of an octagonal cupola (left). The

twin crossed ribbing allows space within the sculpture to fill the whole with heroic figures, cherubim, satyrs and bearded sages. The barrel vaults in the arms of the transept are also bedecked with busts of mythical personages of antiquity, others extolling the deeds of, Gonzalo Fernández de Cordova, King Ferdinand's Gran Capitán, and in the caissons a complete study of anatomy and movement of fanciful figures. Towards the main chapel religious themes are more in evidence: angels with aspects of the Passion, the apostles, the three virtues, the biblical co-existing side by side with the mythical, the whole history of mankind saved by the Passion of Christ, who presides over the altar piece, finally assimilated by Renaissance culture. The choir stalls, also the work of de Siloë, are a Renaissance recital of sensitivity and delicacy and some can be seen in the Museum of Fine Arts in the Alhambra.

THE CARTHUSIAN MONASTERY (LA CARTUJA)

The Carthusian order was founded some nine hundred years ago by St. Bruno and was in fact one of the various reformed monastic orders to spring from the reaction against the spiritual decline of the Cluniac regime. The main innovations of the Carthusian order were silence, isolation and fasting, all of which were perfectly regulated so as not to result in too much physical or mental hardship. The efficiency of their regime was such that it still survives today completely unreformed. Throughout the XV century they had spread themselves widely, particularly through the Iberian peninsula, and their monastic foundations were patronised by kings and grandees who wanted to own a family pantheon. Thus the Car-

thusian monastery in Granada was the foundation which the Gran Capitán decided to build in the hamlet of Ainadamar, *the spring of tears,* on the outskirts of the city during the years immediately after the conquest. But in the end the Carthusians had to build it themselves. Fray Alonso de Ledesma began the initial Gothic structure in 1514, but the work went on long enough for it to be touched by the splendour of the Baroque. Although there is no written rule on the subject, all Carthusian monasteries are built in the same shape, which divides the structure of the monastery into a church with a single nave on one side and on the other, two cloisters with their adjoining rooms. Around the great cloister were large private cells with

their own gardens, all of which have disappeared since the disentailment of the church in 1835. Nowadays only the church and the small cloister remain, around which are grouped the refectory, two chapels and the chapter house. The originality of this monastery is to be found above all in two particular areas that make it unique of its kind: the sac-

risty and the shrine, or sancta sanctorum, where the XVIII century Andalucian Baroque reaches the height of its expressionism. The structure of the church, with its sober exterior, is the cell of Jesus Christ, the first hermit, the monastery's revered guest and its interior decoration must be equal to his splendour. It is also the hub of monasterial life, where the monks may spend up to eight hours a day in prayer. As usual it is composed of three separate sections: at the entrance a choir for laymen, separated by a screen from a second choir devoted to the use of the fathers, and the presbytery, which here is divided into two sections, the main altar and the shrine. It is in this latter small sanctuary that Hurtado Izquierdo managed to capture in marble and gold the post-tridentine idea of the exaltation of the Eucharist. It is only a metaphorical representation, humanity expressed in stone, and thus merely symbolic of eternal glorification. The central niche, or main shrine, designed to contain the body of Christ, is the source from which all life springs and this eschatological concept is manifest in the twin fountains with shells (the symbol of water and life) from whence grace flows (*see opposite page*). Everything in the shrine dazzles; it is the *horror vacui* so characteristic of the Baroque taken to its most uninhibited heights of expression, it offers the eye no escape, envelopes it in a cloud of brilliantly coloured geometric stimuli. The celestial cupola which crowns the whole (*above*), built by Palomino some time during the 1770's, begins with familiar Renaissance, and above all tridentine symbolism, according to which the Holy Trinity presided over the creation of the universe. The figures of the Holy Fathers, the Angels, the Virtues, the Four Apostles (the pillars of the faith) occupy the base of the cupola, gathered around St. Bruno, who holds the terrestrial

globe containing the weight of the sins of mankind, above all of which the Eucharist rises triumphant.

THE SACRISTY

The adjacent sacristy is considered by many experts on the subject to be the last great creation of the Spanish Baroque. This chamber, far from being just one more room in the monastery, is in fact the most important after the church itself, the place where the fathers prepare themselves for the most solemn moment of the day, the communal mass. It is the anteroom to the shrine and is sacred in itself and so it reminds us of a small church only distinguishable from such by its chests adorned with marquetry inlays of marble, silver, mahogany, rosewood, ebony and tortoiseshell, worked on for thirty-four years by Brother Vásquez, in a labour of prayer and devotion. Hurtado Izquierdo paved the floor with bicoloured rhomboids which appear to open outwards, giving the impression of great space and at the same time focusing the attention upon the pilasters and the walls, covered in a multitudinous variety of linear shapes in white stucco, creating the illusion of a pellucid space full of light. Presiding over the sacristy is an altar carved of pink marble from the nearby village of Loja, with the figure of St. Bruno reflecting upon death, and in a niche on the left, a magnificent sculpture by José de Mora of St. Bruno in a state of spiritual ecstasy, full of contained vitality such as no other in the canon of Baroque expressionism and mysticism (*below left*).

Two statues from the small cloister: to the left, The Virgin of Risueño, and right, a terracota Christ by the García brothers.

The Sierra Nevada stretches for some 90 kilometres between Granada and Almería. It is the highest mountain range in the Iberian Peninsula, its loftiest peak, Mulhacen, rising to 3.482 metres. Most of it has been declared a nature reserve to protect its many endemic species of flora and fauna.

The ski resort is just below the second-highest peak, the Veleta. It has the charm of a small skiing village together with all modern conveniences and over 60 kilometres of ski runs to suit all tastes and skills. In summer it is a perfect base for rambling in the high mountains

Frédérique et Pierre Novat

Montefrío

El Fargue

Arriba, Moclín; debajo Salobreña

GRANADA PROVINCE

The geography and countryside of the Province of Granada is widely varied, ranging from the snows of the high mountains to inland meseta plains and the sub-tropical Mediterranean coast. Amidst such diversity it is possible to ski in the morning and swim in the sea in the afternoon. The province comprises seven districts: the Capital City, surrounded by mountains and the fertile plain to the west; Western Granada, with three important towns: Montefrío (above and left), set in impressive rocky countryside interspersed with meadows and the towering Peña de los Gitanos, a stoney scarp containing some interesting prehistoric sites, Loja, known throughout history as "the Gateway to Granada" and Alhama de Granada, with its natural thermal springs and baths. Both these latter towns were important Moorish strongholds before and during the conquest. The first to fall was Alhama and during a skirmish at Loja the last sultan of the Nasrid dynasty, Boabdil, was taken prisoner by the Christians, although it could easily have gone the other way and King Ferdinand could have found himself a prisoner of the Muslims. The medieval castles of both towns still overlook them from the heights of almost inaccessible crags. The third district is that of the Tropical Coast to the south, with seaside towns such as Almuñecar and Salobreña (left and below) and Motril, where the only sugar cane in Europe is still grown, most of it going to make the superb local rum. Other crops to grow in this enviable sub-tropical climate are mangoes, avocados and custard apples. On the southern slopes of the Sierra Nevada is the Alpujarra, a district of mountain villages, so special that it is worth a more detailed account in the following pages. The Sierra Nevada itself forms the fifth district of the province. Almost all of it is a national

MOCLÍN

MONTEFRÍO

GRAN

SANTAFÉ

LOJA

ALHAMA

ALMUÑECAR

park and nature reserve and is home to a large number of endemic species of plants and animals. It also has the southernmost ski resort in Europe. The two remaining districts lie in the north-east of the province and may almost be considered as one, lying

Tózar

as they do on the high Guadix-Baza plain around the dip in the terrain known as the Hoya, which was in recent geological time an inland sea. Archaeologists have discovered here what may be evidence of the first hominids in Europe and the area has certainly been inhabited continuously from earliest prehistoric times. Guadix and Baza were both important Moorish strongholds and the ruins of their fortified Muslim citadels can still be seen today. One of their most curious attractions is the considerable troglodyte population. The cave dwellings of the area can be quite luxurious and the constant, year-round temperature inside them of around 18ºC is very much appreciated by their owners.

Guadix

Not far from Guadix, just beside the road to Almería, in the foothills of the Sierra Nevada, is the castle of La Calahorra *(right and below)*.

Built in 1509 by the grandson of Cardenal Mendoza, the marquis of Zenete, using marble brought from Genoa, it is the first Renaissance building in Spain, even predating the palace of Charles V in the Alhambra. The Catholic Monarchs had clipped the wings of the rebel Castillian nobility, but when Isabel died the nobles once again confronted the widower King Ferdinand in an attempt to retrieve their lost privileges. The incipient rebellion was put down by Cardinal Cisneros. This castle is one of the last extant examples of the waning power of the nobles. Its central courtyard is one of the most beautiful and refined in the Italian XV century style in Spain.

Arriba y abajo, la Calahorra

HUESCAR

BAZA

LÚA DE GUADIX

GUADIX

JARRAS

OTRIL

A

To the left, the village of Bubión. Just below, a map of the Poqueira river valley, and below to the left, the village of Capileira. Overleaf: above, Cájar and below, Trevélez at 1,650 metres

Map labels:
Dúrcal
Nigüelas
Acequias
Tello
Los Caballe
Modujar
Capileira
Lecrín
Bubión
Pórtugos
Murchas
Pampaneira
Pitres
Chite
Soportújar
Lanjarón
Cañar
Mecina
Carataunas
No
Izbor
Órgiva
Los Tablones
Torvi
Alcázar

THE ALPUJARRA

From the heights of the Sierra Nevada one can see Africa, and just down below there is a scattering of white villages built on the sides of steep green valleys that stretch away towards the Guadalfeo river and thence to the sea. A direct view of the sea is interrupted by the silhouette of the last folds of the Sierra Nevada, the Contraviesa hills and the Sierra de Lújar, as though the mountains were loth to fall too quickly into the Mediterranean. These white villages belong to the Alpujarra, a district which because of its geographical inaccessibility has remained isolated for centuries, following a way of life conditioned by its terrain and its own singular history, making it a relic of the past and a present-day jewel. Few places can offer such scenery and human interest for tourists who are looking for contact with nature and the rural way of life.

The impression of isolation one gets in the Alpujarra, more imaginary than real in fact, has even encouraged a group of Buddhist monks to settle there, the landscape probably reminding them somewhat of Tibet with its snowy peaks and wide horizons. The Alpujarra has always been a place for peoples who sought isolation or were fleeing from pursuers. The Berbers, who came out worst in the share out of land during the early Arab occupation of Spain, came here to live in the VIII century and turned it into a vast orchard of fruit trees, especially mulberries for the silk trade. When the conquerors demanded that the Muslims convert to Christianity many of them sought refuge here away from the Inquisition in a place where they could continue to wear their customary clothes, speak their own language and practice their religion in relative peace. But it was from here that

Aben Humeya led the disastrous Muslim revolt against Granada in 1568, which king Phillip II quelled by sending his half-brother Don Juan of Austria to impose the intransigence of the old Christian ways upon the population, and finally to expel most of them from his dominions.

Of the various river valleys that cut through the Alpujarra the best known is that of the Poqueira, with three snowy white villages clinging to its side: Pampaneira, Bubión and Capileira. A few years ago it was possible to cross the Sierra Nevada from the Alpujarra to Granada by way of an unmetalled road that passed just under the peak of the Veleta, making it the highest road in Europe, but now that the area has been declared a national park the road is closed and visitors must come up some of the way by coach and then continue on foot into what must be some of the most rugged and beautiful terrain for mountain

walking in Europe. To continue into the Alpujarra the visitor has to return down the Poqueira valley and turn east along a winding road to enter into the next valley overlooked by the villages of Pitres and Pórtugos, with its natural springs of
 bitter but health-giving ferruginous water. Busquitar can be seen close by but the road is deceitful and manages to make the distance much longer than it seems. At the head of the river valley is Trevélez, rising suddenly like an apparition at the highest point of the road. Its height at 1, 650 metres makes it ideal for curing hams in the cold mountain air, a delicacy which has justly given the village its fame. The microfauna and flora of the area are believed to contain certain organisms, not all of them fully known, which are essential to the process of curing the hams and are the envy of other ham-curing regions, which bring some of their products here in summer for them to "catch" whatever is in the air. Local cooking is of course centred around pork, and pork sausages of all kinds form the basis of many typical Alpujarran dishes, accompanied by fried eggs and potatoes fried with sweet green peppers (patatas a lo pobre).

The vegetation around the villages is varied and often changes abruptly from place to place, depending upon the water that flows down from the rivers, water which is then cleverly routed along irrigation channels and ceramic pipes that the Arabs ins-

talled centuries ago. Lines of oaks and chestnut trees define the boundaries between vegetable gardens and orchards of fruit trees, some of which appear to be defying gravity, perched on the sides of the steepest banks of the valley (above). The surrounding rocks and trees have always been the raw material for village houses, and the art of building with them has been refined down the years. The houses themselves are built from dry-stone, and slates from the mountainside are then used to cover the walnut and chestnut roof-beams. The flat roof is then sealed with grey, powdered-slate clay to make the typical terrao, where grapes and figs are dried while red peppers and corn cobs hang from the balconies amongst a profusion of geraniums, pinks and carnations, bedecking the whitewashed walls with startling arrays of colour. Runnels of water still flow down the middle of narrow winding streets, living examples of the architecture brought here from Africa by the Berbers over a thousand years ago. Almost all the houses face south to capture as much of the winter sun as they can, whilst their wide eaves protect them from the extreme summer heat. At this height there is no barrier to prevent warm breezes blowing in from the Mediterranean some fifty kilometres to the south, and behind these villages the high sierra helps to cool the worst of the heat in summer, thus giving them a moderate, benign climate throughout most of the year.

La segunda parte de este libro "LA GRANADA CRISTIANA" ha sido reelaborada en los talleres de Edilux s.l. y se acabó de imprimir en Copartgraf el día del Corpus de 2002.
©Texto y edición: Edilux.
© Dibujos infográficos de la Catedral: Juan Manuel Fernández Linares de MAMANI PRODUCCIONES, S.L.
Fotografías digitales: Miguel Román

Tratamiento de las imágenes: Pablo Román
Supervisión: Julia Avigliano
Edilux agradece a los cabildos de la Capilla Real y de la Catedral la ayuda prestada y especialmente al profesor Dr. D. Juan Manuel Gómez Segade por su colaboración.
Distribución: Edilux, s.l. (telf. 958-082000)
E.mail: ediluxsl@supercable.es